Mainframe Processing: Principles and Paradigms

CW00503226

Ricardo Nuqui

Mainframe Knowledge

Published by Nuqui Ricardo Regala, 2023

While every precaution has been taken in the preparation of this book, the publisher assumes no responsibility for errors or omissions, or for damages resulting from the use of the information contained herein.

MAINFRAME TRANSACTION PROCESSING: PRINCIPLES, PRACTICES, AND PARADIGMS

First edition. June 11, 2023.

ISBN: 978-9815164893

Written by Ricardo Nuqui.

Table of Contents

To Coleen, Sky and Neo. You are my inspirations.

Preface

In an era that prides itself on the newest innovations, it is easy to forget the foundations upon which these breakthroughs are built. The world of information technology is no exception. Amid the excitement around emerging technologies, mainframes have stood the test of time, proving their relevance and resilience time and again. As the backbone of global industries, mainframes handle large-scale transaction processing with remarkable efficiency and unparalleled reliability.

"Mainframe Transaction Processing: Principles, Practices, and Paradigms" aims to provide readers a comprehensive guide to the world of mainframe transaction processing. The aim is to shed light on the crucial role that mainframes play in modern businesses and industries and to unravel the complexity of transaction processing systems.

The book is designed to be informative for a wide range of readers. It provides a fundamental understanding for beginners and simultaneously delves into advanced concepts for seasoned professionals seeking to enhance their knowledge.

The initial chapters introduce mainframes and transaction processing, offering historical context and an overview of their modern applications. Subsequent chapters provide a deeper dive into the operating systems, databases, and programming languages relevant to mainframe transaction processing.

An entire section is dedicated to the architecture and lifecycle of transaction processing, discussing the security considerations and performance optimization techniques. The book does not shy away from discussing the future of mainframes, addressing emerging trends and how they are likely to shape transaction processing systems.

One of the unique aspects of this book is its focus on practical application. Real-world case studies are included to demonstrate the power and potential of mainframe transaction processing. The aim is to go beyond theory, illustrating how mainframes are used in real-world scenarios, driving some of the world's largest and most successful organizations.

As you journey through this book, it is my hope that you will gain a comprehensive understanding of mainframe transaction processing. Whether you are a student, a professional, or a curious individual, I hope this book will deepen your understanding, spark your interest, and fuel your passion for the fascinating world of mainframes.

Thank you for choosing to explore this exciting domain with "Mainframe Transaction Processing: Principles, Practices, and Paradigms". Happy reading!

Ricardo Nuqui

Prologue

===

I n the early 1950s, when the first commercial computers started to emerge, few could have imagined the profound transformation they would bring about in the following decades. These pioneering machines were nothing short of technological marvels, yet they were also cumbersome, expensive, and limited in their capabilities by today's standards.

Among these early computing giants, the mainframes emerged, powerful machines capable of managing enormous amounts of data and processing transactions at a scale unheard of before. These systems, with their unrivaled power, would serve as the backbone for countless industries and enterprises worldwide.

Over the years, as newer, smaller, and more agile computing technologies were developed, many predicted the demise of the mainframe. They argued that such massive, resource-intensive systems would be supplanted by more modern technologies. Yet, mainframes have not only survived but continue to thrive, playing a crucial role in our global digital infrastructure. Today, they are the silent workhorses behind global finance, insurance, healthcare, transportation, and numerous other sectors.

The essence of the mainframe's enduring success lies in its ability to process transactions on a massive scale reliably, securely, and efficiently. But what exactly does this mean? What is a "transaction," and why is the process so important that it warrants an entire book?

Imagine you're at an ATM. You insert your card, punch in your pin, request cash, and receive the money. That entire interaction, from start to finish, constitutes a transaction. Now, imagine millions of such transactions happening simultaneously, each needing to be processed accurately and securely—that's the realm of mainframe transaction processing.

This book, "Mainframe Transaction Processing: Principles, Practices, and Paradigms," aims to delve into the very heart of the mainframe's enduring relevance. We'll explore the processes, techniques, and technologies that allow these venerable machines to handle the world's transaction processing needs.

As we embark on this journey, we'll discover that the mainframe, far from being a relic of the past, is a vibrant, evolving technology. It is adapting to new paradigms, such as cloud computing and AI, while maintaining the core qualities that made it indispensable in the first place.

The road ahead promises to be a journey of discovery. It's a journey that will take us into the heart of the digital world's transactional pulse, the mainframe. So, buckle up and enjoy the ride!

Introduction to the Book

———

Welcome to "Mainframe Transaction Processing: Principles, Practices, and Paradigms" – a comprehensive guide into the complex and captivating world of mainframe systems and their role in transaction processing. This book has been carefully curated to provide a detailed, understandable, and insightful look at this significant aspect of modern information technology.

We live in a digital age defined by transactions. Every time we withdraw money from an ATM, make a purchase online, book a flight, or even like a post on social media, we initiate transactions that need to be processed reliably and securely. The scale at which these transactions are managed today is mind-boggling and at the heart of this colossal infrastructure are mainframe systems.

Mainframes have been an integral part of our digital ecosystem since their inception. Their ability to handle large-scale, complex transactions with unmatched reliability has made them indispensable in various industries, including banking, healthcare, transportation, and retail. In spite of the advent of newer technologies, mainframes continue to be relevant, holding their ground as a vital element of global IT systems.

In this book, we will delve deep into the world of mainframe transaction processing, starting from the basics and advancing to more complex concepts. We will explore how mainframes are engineered, how they process transactions, and how they have evolved to meet the changing demands of the digital age.

"Mainframe Transaction Processing" is divided into seven parts. The initial part focuses on the fundamentals of mainframes and transaction processing, providing a solid foundation for readers new to the subject. The following sections dive into the specifics of mainframe operating systems, programming languages, and databases involved in transaction processing.

The book further explores the architecture and lifecycle of transaction processing, discussing in detail the security and performance aspects vital to these systems. Future trends and advanced transactional models in mainframes are covered, giving readers an insight into the evolution of this technology.

One of the book's unique features is its focus on practical applications and case studies, connecting theory with real-world scenarios. By the end, you'll not only understand how mainframe transaction processing works but also see how it drives successful businesses worldwide.

Whether you're an IT professional wanting to broaden your knowledge, a student learning about mainframe systems, or a technology enthusiast curious about the backbone of our digital world, this book aims to be a valuable resource.

We welcome you to "Mainframe Transaction Processing: Principles, Practices, and Paradigms". Let's embark on this exciting journey together.

Part I: Fundamentals of Mainframes and Transaction Processing

———

Welcome to the first section of "Mainframe Transaction Processing: Principles, Practices, and Paradigms" – Fundamentals of Mainframes and Transaction Processing. This part of the book lays the foundation for understanding the complex world of mainframes and the intricate process of transaction management they handle so adeptly.

Our exploration begins with a broad overview of mainframes, dissecting their historical context, their key characteristics, and the unique value they offer in today's technology landscape. The aim is to paint a picture of the integral role mainframes have played in shaping our digital world and their enduring relevance despite the rapid evolution of technology.

From there, we'll delve into the concept of transaction processing. What constitutes a transaction? Why is its processing so crucial to modern business operations? How do these transactions take place in a digital environment? These are some of the questions we will address as we demystify the nature of digital transactions.

Next, we explore the place of mainframes in our modern world. Although mainframes have been around for several decades, they continue to adapt to changing technological landscapes, handling workloads that other systems simply cannot manage. This chapter will highlight the evolving role of mainframes and why they continue to be indispensable.

This section serves as an essential stepping stone, providing you with the necessary grounding to appreciate and understand the more technical and advanced concepts discussed later in the book. Whether you are completely new to this field or just need a quick refresher, these initial chapters aim to bring you up to speed and ready for the detailed exploration that follows.

As we embark on this journey through the world of mainframes and transaction processing, it is our hope that you will gain not just knowledge, but also an appreciation for these remarkable systems that silently power our digital world. Enjoy the journey!

Chapter 1: Overview of Mainframes

1.1 The Genesis of Mainframes

The story of mainframes begins in the mid-20th century, when these colossal machines were conceived to tackle complex calculations and data processing tasks. The chapter traces the origin and evolution of mainframes, discussing early models and the technological advancements that led to the mainframes we see today.

1.2 Characteristics of Mainframes

Mainframes are distinguished by certain unique characteristics. This section explains these features, which include their large size, significant processing power, high level of reliability, exceptional security, and capability to handle vast amounts of data and concurrent transactions.

1.3 Mainframe Architecture

At the heart of every mainframe is its architecture, the blueprint that defines its structure and operation. This part explores the hardware and software components of mainframe architecture, providing a broad understanding of how these systems are designed and how they function.

1.4 Mainframe Operating Systems

Over the years, various operating systems have been developed specifically for mainframes to leverage their power and efficiency. This section delves into the world of mainframe operating systems, discussing popular ones like z/OS, z/VM, z/VSE, and Linux on IBM Z.

1.5 Types of Mainframes

Not all mainframes are created equal. There are different types of mainframes, each designed to serve specific needs. This section explains the different classes of mainframes, from System/360 to the modern IBM Z series, and the use-cases they are designed to handle.

1.6 Roles and Applications of Mainframes

Mainframes play a crucial role in many industries, handling a range of applications that require substantial processing power and reliability. This part covers the various roles and applications of mainframes in sectors such as banking, healthcare, retail, transportation, and government.

1.7 The Myth of Mainframe Obsolescence

Despite being older technology, mainframes are far from obsolete. This section dispels the myth of mainframe obsolescence, explaining why these powerful systems continue to be relevant and vital in today's fast-paced digital world.

This chapter aims to provide a comprehensive understanding of mainframes, their architecture, their capabilities, and their applications. By the end of this chapter, you should have a well-rounded view of what mainframes are and why they continue to be indispensable assets in our digital economy.

1.1 The Genesis of Mainframes

MAINFRAMES, LIKE MOST computing technology, have their roots in the scientific and military research efforts of the mid-20th century. Their genesis traces back to a time when computers were enormous machines, housed in large rooms, and operated by teams of specialists.

The journey began in the 1950s when IBM, a key player in the mainframe industry, launched its first commercially available computer, the IBM 701. The 701 was a behemoth, primarily designed for scientific calculations. However, it wasn't until the introduction of the IBM System/360 in 1964 that the term "mainframe" started being widely used. The System/360 was revolutionary; it offered a suite of compatible models with different performance levels and prices, but all capable of running the same software.

The 360 set the standard for what would be expected from mainframes. It offered businesses a powerful tool to process large volumes of transactions and data, which became particularly valuable with the increasing digitization of business records and processes.

The evolution of mainframes continued through the 70s and 80s, with significant advancements in processing power, storage capacity, and system architecture. IBM introduced the System/370 in 1970, which added virtual memory capabilities. Later came the System/390 in the 1990s, which dramatically increased processing power and introduced a more advanced, secure, and reliable system architecture.

Throughout this period, mainframes faced competition from the rise of smaller, cheaper mini-computers and later from microcomputers (PCs). But mainframes held their ground by providing unparalleled transaction processing capabilities, which made them invaluable to large enterprises such as banks, insurance companies, airlines, and government agencies.

In the early 21st century, the IBM Z series represented a major step forward, offering even more processing power, higher levels of system integrity, and advanced features for e-business. The introduction of Linux on mainframes during this period also opened new avenues for mainframe applications, ensuring their ongoing relevance in an ever-evolving technology landscape.

The story of mainframes is one of continued evolution and adaptation. These powerful machines have consistently managed to reinvent themselves to meet the changing needs of businesses and organizations. From the IBM 701 to the IBM Z series, mainframes have transitioned from being room-sized behemoths to becoming highly sophisticated, compact, and powerful systems that continue to form the backbone of global business operations.

As we move forward in this book, we'll explore in more depth how mainframes work, why they are so powerful, and why, after over six decades, they continue to be an integral part of our global IT infrastructure.

1.2 Characteristics of Mainframes

MAINFRAMES HAVE A SET of distinct features that set them apart from other computer systems and make them the technology of choice for many critical business operations.

1.2.1 Large Size and Scalability

Mainframes are renowned for their large size and their ability to scale. Traditional mainframes could occupy entire rooms, although modern ones have significantly reduced in physical size while increasing in computational capacity. The scalability of mainframes is one of their standout features. They can handle an increase in workload by adding more processors, memory, or storage, allowing organizations to scale up their operations without having to replace or overhaul their existing systems.

1.2.2 Processing Power

Mainframes are powerhouses when it comes to processing capabilities. They can handle billions of simple computations per second, making them ideal for large-scale, transaction-intensive operations. This is particularly crucial for industries such as banking, retail, and logistics, where huge volumes of transactions occur daily.

1.2.3 High Reliability

Mainframes are built to deliver high reliability, availability, and serviceability (RAS). They are designed to avoid single points of failure, have redundancy built into their hardware components, and provide sophisticated error checking and recovery capabilities. This means they can achieve near-continuous uptime, which is a critical requirement for many businesses.

1.2.4 Exceptional Security

Security is a primary concern for any computing system, but it's even more critical for mainframes, which often handle sensitive and valuable data. Mainframes offer a variety of security features, from encryption and access controls to intrusion detection and auditing capabilities. They also support multi-factor authentication and have unique hardware features that help protect data even when it's being processed.

1.2.5 Concurrent Processing and Throughput

One of the key strengths of mainframes is their ability to handle a large number of concurrent transactions. They can execute thousands of tasks at the same time, making them ideal for situations where many users need to access and manipulate data simultaneously. This is often referred to as "throughput" - the amount of work a computer can handle over a given period.

1.2.6 Efficient Resource Management

Mainframes are designed to make the most efficient use of their resources, including processors, memory, and storage. They employ sophisticated scheduling algorithms to ensure that all tasks are given the appropriate amount of processing time and that system resources are used effectively. This efficient resource management is crucial for achieving high performance and is part of what makes mainframes so cost-effective for large-scale operations.

In essence, the distinguishing characteristics of mainframes lie in their power, reliability, security, and efficiency. These qualities have allowed mainframes to stand the test of time and continue to be a crucial part of the IT infrastructure in many industries.

1.3 Mainframe Architecture

THE ARCHITECTURE OF a mainframe refers to its overall design and the relationship between its various components. Understanding the architecture is crucial to appreciating how mainframes can handle such vast amounts of data and transactions with exceptional speed, reliability, and security.

1.3.1 Hardware Architecture

The hardware components of a mainframe are meticulously engineered to ensure optimal performance, reliability, and scalability. Key elements include:

- Central Processing Units (CPUs): Mainframes typically have multiple CPUs (also known as cores or processors) that can operate independently or cooperatively to execute instructions. Each CPU can run multiple threads simultaneously, enabling a high degree of parallel processing.
- Memory: Mainframes use a hierarchical memory structure, consisting of cache, main storage (RAM), and auxiliary storage. This structure allows them to manage large amounts of data efficiently. Main storage in mainframes can extend to several terabytes, ensuring that large databases and applications can be held in memory for faster processing.
- Channels and Control Units: Channels are specialized processors dedicated to input/output (I/O) operations. They communicate with peripheral devices like disk drives and tape drives through control units. This architecture allows the CPUs to delegate I/O operations to the

channels, freeing them to focus on computation.

- Storage Devices: These include both internal and external storage devices, such as hard drives, solid-state drives, and tape drives. Modern mainframes also support connections to networked storage systems.

1.3.2 Software Architecture

The software architecture of a mainframe is layered and modular, allowing for high flexibility and adaptability. Key elements include:

- Operating System: The operating system (OS) is the core software that manages hardware resources and provides services for other software to run. Common mainframe OSes include z/OS, z/VM, z/VSE, and Linux on IBM Z.
- Middleware: This is the software layer that sits between the OS and the application software. It provides useful services such as transaction processing, database management, and message queuing, helping to simplify the development and operation of applications.
- Application Software: These are the programs that perform the actual business functions, such as transaction processing systems, enterprise resource planning (ERP) systems, and customer relationship management (CRM) systems.

The mainframe architecture's design allows for efficient resource use, high-speed processing, concurrent execution of multiple tasks, and robust security. It's this thoughtful architecture that enables mainframes to process millions of transactions per day and support the mission-critical operations of global enterprises.

1.4 Mainframe Operating Systems

THE OPERATING SYSTEM (OS) of a mainframe is critical to its performance and functionality. Over the years, several operating systems have been developed specifically for mainframes, each designed to make the most of their capabilities.

1.4.1 z/OS

z/OS is the flagship operating system for IBM Z mainframes. It's designed for enterprise computing and excels at handling large-scale, high-volume transaction processing. z/OS offers robust security features, sophisticated workload management capabilities, and strong support for various middleware and database systems. Its advanced features include Parallel Sysplex, which enables the clustering of mainframes for high availability and scalability.

1.4.2 z/VM

z/VM is a highly secure and scalable virtualization operating system for IBM Z mainframes. Its primary function is to run multiple virtual machines that can each host their own guest operating system. This makes z/VM an excellent choice for consolidating workloads on a single mainframe, reducing hardware costs, and increasing efficiency.

1.4.3 z/VSE

z/VSE (Virtual Storage Extended) is designed for smaller mainframe environments. While not as feature-rich as z/OS, it's a reliable and cost-effective solution for running batch and transaction processing workloads. z/VSE supports a range of IBM and third-party middleware, allowing users to extend its functionality as needed.

1.4.4 Linux on IBM Z

In recent years, Linux has become an increasingly popular choice for mainframe operating systems. Linux on IBM Z combines the open-source flexibility and wide software availability of Linux with the power and reliability of IBM's mainframe hardware. It's particularly well-suited for running modern, open-source software stacks, making it an attractive choice for enterprises looking to leverage mainframes for newer applications such as big data analytics and cloud services.

Each of these operating systems brings its unique strengths and features to the table. The choice of OS will depend on various factors, including the nature of the workloads to be run, the need for specific features or support for certain software, the available budget, and the organization's long-term IT strategy. Regardless of the choice, the operating system will play a crucial role in harnessing the power of the mainframe and adapting it to the organization's needs.

1.5 Types of Mainframes

OVER THE DECADES, MAINFRAME designs have evolved to meet changing technology needs and business requirements. There are several notable classes of mainframes, each with its specific features and strengths:

1.5.1 System/360

Launched in the 1960s, the IBM System/360 was a game-changer. It introduced the concept of a complete series of compatible systems, each offering varying performance levels but all able to run the same software. System/360 machines were large, physically imposing systems that found use in many large-scale industries and scientific research.

1.5.2 System/370

The IBM System/370, introduced in 1970, brought enhancements over the System/360, notably the addition of virtual memory, which allowed for more efficient use of system resources and simplified programming. This system was designed to handle a wide range of tasks, from large-scale business and scientific applications to smaller, departmental workloads.

1.5.3 System/390

Unveiled in the early 1990s, the System/390 represented a significant leap in processing power and system capacity. It introduced the Enterprise Systems Architecture/390 (ESA/390), which expanded the system's addressing capability and introduced a host of advanced features, such as integrated cryptography for enhanced security.

1.5.4 zSeries

The zSeries, later renamed to IBM Z, marks IBM's entry into the 21st-century mainframe market. The zSeries introduced the z/Architecture, which further expanded the system's addressing capability to support even larger databases and transaction volumes. Subsequent models have brought improvements in processing power, energy efficiency, and physical compactness, along with enhanced virtualization and encryption capabilities.

1.5.5 IBM LinuxONE

IBM LinuxONE is a dedicated Linux and open-source mainframe solution that's based on IBM Z technology. It's designed to provide a highly secure, scalable, and reliable environment for deploying a wide range of Linux and open-source software, offering a compelling blend of traditional mainframe strengths with modern software capabilities.

Each of these mainframe classes has its unique features and capabilities. However, they all share the core mainframe principles of high performance, reliability, security, and scalability. Whether it's the venerable System/360 or the cutting-edge IBM Z, mainframes continue to serve as the digital backbone for numerous industries and enterprises worldwide.

1.6 Roles and Applications of Mainframes

DESPITE ADVANCEMENTS in other forms of computing, mainframes remain indispensable in many sectors due to their unmatched reliability, processing power, and data handling capabilities. Let's explore some key roles and applications of mainframes in various sectors.

1.6.1 Banking and Financial Services

Mainframes play a crucial role in the banking and financial industry. They handle core banking systems, credit card transactions, stock exchange transactions, and insurance claims processing, among other tasks. Given the high-volume, high-value, and highly sensitive nature of these transactions, the reliability, security, and processing power of mainframes make them the preferred choice for these operations.

1.6.2 Healthcare

In the healthcare sector, mainframes are used to manage patient records, billing systems, and insurance claim databases. They also support critical research applications, crunching vast amounts of data for epidemiological studies, drug discovery, and genomics.

1.6.3 Retail

Mainframes support point-of-sale transactions, inventory management, supply chain management, and customer relationship management systems in the retail sector. During peak shopping times, such as Black Friday and Cyber Monday, mainframes ensure these systems remain available and responsive despite the high transaction volumes.

1.6.4 Transportation

In the transportation sector, mainframes manage reservation systems, logistics and cargo tracking systems, and customer loyalty programs. Airlines, for example, rely on mainframes to process millions of bookings and check-ins each day and to ensure smooth operations.

1.6.5 Government

Government agencies use mainframes for a wide range of applications, including tax processing, social services programs, defense and intelligence work, and managing census data. The scalability, security, and reliability of mainframes are critical for these large-scale, often sensitive operations.

In essence, mainframes underpin the IT infrastructure of numerous industries, ensuring smooth, secure, and efficient operations. Their role in processing and managing vast amounts of data quickly and reliably is a testament to their enduring relevance in the digital age. As we continue to generate more data and digital transactions, the role of mainframes will likely remain critical in supporting our increasingly digital economies and societies.

1.7 The Myth of Mainframe Obsolescence

MAINFRAMES HAVE BEEN a part of the IT landscape for over half a century, leading some to believe they are obsolete in today's era of cloud computing, microservices, and agile methodologies. However, this couldn't be further from the truth. While they are indeed mature technology, mainframes have evolved significantly over the years and continue to play a critical role in modern business operations.

1.7.1 Continual Evolution

One key factor that contradicts the myth of mainframe obsolescence is their continual evolution. Companies like IBM have consistently invested in upgrading mainframe technology to keep pace with changing business needs and technological advancements. From enhancing processing power to introducing new features like advanced virtualization and pervasive encryption, mainframe technology has never stood still.

1.7.2 Unmatched Capabilities

Mainframes offer several unique capabilities that remain unmatched by other technologies. They can process huge volumes of transactions quickly and securely, making them indispensable for industries like banking, retail, and healthcare. They provide near-uninterrupted uptime, which is a crucial requirement for mission-critical applications. Additionally, they offer efficient resource utilization and can handle diverse and concurrent workloads, contributing to lower total cost of ownership in high-volume environments.

1.7.3 Modern Integration

Today's mainframes can run modern software, and they support web technologies, API interfaces, and open-source software. IBM's LinuxONE and Linux on IBM Z platforms, for instance, marry the robustness and scalability of mainframes with the flexibility and wide application support of Linux. Furthermore, mainframes can be seamlessly integrated with cloud architectures, allowing businesses to leverage the strengths of both technologies.

1.7.4 Skills Availability

While there's some concern about the availability of skills for mainframe systems, initiatives are in place to address this. Universities, vocational schools, and companies like IBM offer courses on mainframe programming and administration. Furthermore, thanks to the integration of mainframes with modern technologies, developers can use familiar languages and tools, like Java, Python, and Git, to work with mainframe systems.

In conclusion, the perception of mainframes as obsolete technology is a myth. Mainframes have evolved and adapted to the changing IT landscape, and they continue to play a vital role in modern enterprise computing. As we move into the future, mainframes will likely remain a cornerstone of IT infrastructure, supporting the ever-growing demand for reliable, secure, high-volume transaction processing.

Chapter 2: Fundamentals of Transaction Processing

———

2.1 Introduction to Transaction Processing

This section introduces transaction processing, explaining what a transaction is, the types of transactions, and why they are crucial for modern businesses. It lays the groundwork for understanding the complex world of transaction processing on mainframes.

2.2 Properties of Transactions

This part delves into the essential properties of transactions, often known by the acronym ACID (Atomicity, Consistency, Isolation, and Durability). Understanding these properties is fundamental to designing and implementing robust transaction processing systems.

2.3 Transaction Processing Systems

Here we examine transaction processing systems, which are software applications designed to handle transactions. We look at their key components, how they work, and the different types of transaction processing systems, such as online transaction processing (OLTP) and batch processing systems.

2.4 Transaction Processing Monitors

Transaction processing monitors (also known as transaction managers or transaction servers) play a vital role in managing and coordinating transactions. This section explores their function, how they ensure the ACID properties of transactions, and some examples of transaction processing monitors used on mainframes.

2.5 Concurrency Control in Transactions

One of the significant challenges in transaction processing is concurrency control, or how to manage multiple transactions happening at the same time. This part explains the problem and explores techniques used to manage concurrency, such as locking, timestamping, and optimistic concurrency control.

2.6 Transaction Recovery

Despite the best precautions, transactions can sometimes fail. This section discusses how transaction processing systems recover from failures, ensuring that the system remains consistent and data is not lost or corrupted.

2.7 Security in Transaction Processing

Transactions often involve sensitive data, so security is paramount. This part discusses the security challenges in transaction processing and the techniques used to address them, such as encryption, secure protocols, and access controls.

2.8 Role of Mainframes in Transaction Processing

Finally, we return to mainframes, discussing why they are uniquely suited to handle high-volume transaction processing and the benefits they bring to transaction processing systems.

2.1 Introduction to Transaction Processing

IN THE DIGITAL WORLD, a vast number of operations occur as transactions - a series of actions carried out as a single, indivisible operation. Be it transferring funds from a bank account, purchasing a product online, or booking an airline ticket, these operations are processed as transactions.

2.1.1 What is a Transaction?

In the context of computing, a transaction is a logical unit of work that consists of one or more related tasks executed as a single operation. It's usually initiated by a user or an application, and it represents a change in the state of a system.

A transaction has two possible outcomes: it can either be completed successfully, in which case all changes are permanently applied to the system, or it can fail, in which case all changes are rolled back, and the system is left in its original state. This all-or-nothing principle ensures data integrity even in the face of system failures.

2.1.2 Types of Transactions

Transactions can be categorized broadly into two types: interactive (or online) transactions and batch transactions.

- Interactive Transactions: These transactions are initiated by a user and occur in real-time. They typically involve a small amount of data and need to be processed quickly. Examples include withdrawing cash from an ATM, making an online purchase, or updating a record in a database.
- Batch Transactions: These transactions are collected and processed as a group or batch, often at scheduled times. Batch transactions are common in environments where

large volumes of similar transactions need to be processed, and immediate response is not critical. Examples include processing payroll for a company, updating inventory records, or generating monthly account statements.

2.1.3 Importance of Transactions in Modern Businesses

Transactions form the backbone of modern business operations. They ensure that data remains consistent and valid, even when multiple users are accessing and modifying it simultaneously. They also help maintain data integrity in the face of system failures or errors.

Moreover, transactions enable businesses to manage complex operations involving multiple steps, ensuring that these operations either complete successfully as a whole or not at all. This ability is critical in many industries, such as banking, retail, and airline reservations, where data accuracy is paramount, and errors can have significant consequences.

In the world of mainframes, transaction processing is a core function. Mainframes excel at processing large volumes of transactions quickly, reliably, and securely, making them an ideal platform for running transaction-intensive applications. As we delve deeper into this chapter, we'll explore the various aspects of transaction processing and how mainframes manage this crucial operation.

2.2 Properties of Transactions

TO ENSURE DATA INTEGRITY and reliability in transaction processing systems, transactions must adhere to certain properties, collectively known as ACID (Atomicity, Consistency, Isolation, Durability). Let's explore each of these properties in detail:

2.2.1 Atomicity

Atomicity refers to the "all-or-nothing" principle of transactions. This means that a transaction is treated as a single, indivisible unit of work, which either completes entirely or not at all. If a transaction is interrupted (for example, due to a system failure or an error), all changes made during that transaction are rolled back, and the system is returned to its original state.

2.2.2 Consistency

Consistency ensures that a transaction brings a system from one valid state to another. This means that before and after a transaction, all data in the system must satisfy a defined set of rules or constraints, known as integrity constraints. If a transaction would violate these constraints, it is rolled back, maintaining the system's consistency.

2.2.3 Isolation

Isolation means that each transaction operates in a manner as if it's the only transaction being processed, even when multiple transactions are executing concurrently. This property ensures that the intermediate state of a transaction is not visible to other transactions. Furthermore, the effects of a completed transaction are immediately visible to new transactions. Isolation is critical for preventing conflicts and inconsistencies when multiple transactions try to access or modify the same data simultaneously.

2.2.4 Durability

Durability guarantees that once a transaction is completed successfully, its effects are permanent and survive any subsequent system failures. This property is often ensured by logging transaction operations to a durable medium (like a disk) and implementing recovery mechanisms.

The ACID properties are a foundational concept in transaction processing, ensuring data integrity, reliability, and robustness. These properties are particularly crucial in mainframe environments, where large volumes of critical transactions are processed, and where even minor errors can have significant repercussions.

2.3 Transaction Processing Systems

TRANSACTION PROCESSING systems (TPS) are computerized systems that perform and record daily routine transactions necessary in the conduct of business. They serve as the backbone of an organization's operations, ensuring that business activities are carried out smoothly, accurately, and reliably.

2.3.1 Key Components of a Transaction Processing System

A transaction processing system typically comprises the following key components:

- Input and Output Interfaces: The system needs mechanisms for receiving transaction requests (input) and delivering transaction results (output). These interfaces can be designed for human users, such as web or mobile interfaces, or for other software systems, such as APIs.
- Transaction Manager: This component, often known as a transaction processing monitor, coordinates the execution of transactions. It ensures the ACID properties of transactions and manages resources like processors, memory, and connections.
- Database Management System (DBMS): The DBMS is responsible for storing and retrieving data. It ensures data consistency and integrity, supports concurrency control, and provides mechanisms for transaction recovery.
- Transaction Log: The transaction log is a record of all transactions and the changes they make to the database. It's a crucial component for ensuring the durability of transactions and for recovering from system failures.

2.3.2 Working of a Transaction Processing System

When a transaction request is received, the transaction manager begins the transaction, coordinating the necessary resources. It communicates with the DBMS to execute the transaction steps, which may involve reading from or writing to the database.

Throughout the transaction, the transaction manager ensures the ACID properties. For instance, it may use locks or timestamps for concurrency control (ensuring isolation), and it rolls back transactions if errors occur (ensuring atomicity).

When a transaction is completed, the transaction manager commits the changes, making them permanent. The DBMS updates the database, and the transaction manager records the transaction in the log (ensuring durability).

2.3.3 Types of Transaction Processing Systems

There are primarily two types of transaction processing systems: Online Transaction Processing (OLTP) systems and Batch Processing systems.

- Online Transaction Processing (OLTP): OLTP systems handle transactions in real-time. They are designed to support a large number of short, interactive transactions where the results are immediately returned to the user. Examples of OLTP systems include ATMs, airline reservation systems, and e-commerce platforms.
- Batch Processing Systems: In batch processing systems, transactions are collected over a period and processed all at once. These systems are used when large amounts of data need to be processed, and there's no need for immediate feedback. Examples include payroll processing, billing systems, and data analysis tasks.

In conclusion, transaction processing systems play a crucial role in modern businesses, enabling them to handle large volumes of transactions quickly, accurately, and reliably. Whether it's processing customer orders, managing bank transactions, or updating airline reservations, these systems ensure that business operations run smoothly and efficiently.

2.4 Transaction Processing Monitors

TRANSACTION PROCESSING Monitors, often referred to as transaction managers or transaction servers, are crucial components of a transaction processing system. They act as the intermediary between client applications and resources such as databases, managing and coordinating the execution of transactions.

2.4.1 Function of a Transaction Processing Monitor

The primary role of a transaction processing monitor is to control the execution of transactions. This involves several responsibilities:

- Resource Management: The monitor manages system resources, such as processors, memory, and connections, ensuring that they're used efficiently and without conflicts.
- Concurrency Control: The monitor manages the simultaneous execution of multiple transactions, ensuring that they don't interfere with each other and maintaining the isolation property of transactions.
- Transaction Scheduling: The monitor determines the order in which transactions are executed, based on factors such as their priority, their dependencies, and system load.
- Failure Recovery: If a transaction fails, the monitor can roll it back to a safe state and retry it, ensuring atomicity and durability of transactions.

2.4.2 Ensuring ACID Properties

The transaction processing monitor plays a key role in maintaining the ACID properties of transactions:

- Atomicity: The monitor ensures that each transaction is

treated as a single, indivisible unit. If a transaction fails at any point, the monitor can roll back all its changes.

- Consistency: By controlling access to resources and managing transaction execution, the monitor helps maintain the consistency of the system's state.

- Isolation: The monitor uses techniques such as locking and timestamping to manage concurrent transactions, ensuring that they don't interfere with each other.

- Durability: The monitor records completed transactions in a durable log, ensuring that their changes are not lost even in the event of a system failure.

2.4.3 Transaction Processing Monitors in Mainframes

Mainframes use robust transaction processing monitors to manage their high-volume, high-speed transaction processing workloads. For instance, IBM's CICS (Customer Information Control System) is a well-known transaction processing monitor used in mainframe environments. CICS supports millions of transactions per second, providing high performance, reliability, and security.

In summary, the transaction processing monitor is a vital component of a transaction processing system, ensuring that transactions are executed efficiently, reliably, and correctly. Whether it's an ATM withdrawal, an online purchase, or a flight booking, behind the scenes, a transaction processing monitor is working to make these operations run smoothly.

2.5 Concurrency Control in Transactions

CONCURRENCY CONTROL is a critical aspect of transaction processing. With multiple transactions executing simultaneously, a system needs mechanisms to ensure that these transactions don't interfere with each other, preserving the integrity of the data and maintaining the isolation property of transactions. Let's dive into the concept of concurrency control and some popular techniques used to achieve it.

2.5.1 The Problem of Concurrency

In a concurrent transaction processing environment, multiple transactions are often accessing and modifying the same data simultaneously. This can lead to several problems:

- Lost Updates: If two transactions read the same data and then update it based on the read value, one transaction's update could be lost.
- Uncommitted Dependency (Dirty Reads): One transaction might read data that another transaction has modified but not yet committed. If the second transaction is then rolled back, the first transaction has read "dirty" data.
- Inconsistent Retrievals: A transaction might read several data items that another transaction is updating concurrently. This can result in inconsistent or incorrect data being read.

2.5.2 Locking

Locking is a common technique for managing concurrency. When a transaction wants to access a data item, it must first acquire a lock on that item. There are two types of locks:

- Shared (Read) Lock: Several transactions can hold a shared lock on a data item simultaneously, but they can only read the data, not modify it.
- Exclusive (Write) Lock: Only one transaction can hold an exclusive lock on a data item, and it can both read and modify the data.

Locking can effectively prevent lost updates, dirty reads, and inconsistent retrievals, but it must be managed carefully to avoid problems like deadlocks, where two or more transactions are each waiting for the other to release a lock.

2.5.3 Timestamping

Timestamping is another technique for managing concurrency. Each transaction is assigned a timestamp when it starts, and the system uses these timestamps to determine the order in which data access requests should be processed. If a transaction wants to read or write a data item that a later transaction has already accessed, the system can deny the request, preventing conflicts.

2.5.4 Optimistic Concurrency Control

Optimistic Concurrency Control (OCC) is a method used in environments where conflicts are relatively rare. Transactions are allowed to proceed without acquiring locks. However, before a transaction can commit, the system checks whether any conflicts have occurred. If a conflict is detected, the transaction is rolled back and retried.

2.5.5 Concurrency Control in Mainframes

Mainframes, with their capability to handle large volumes of transactions concurrently, rely heavily on advanced concurrency control mechanisms. Transaction processing systems like CICS employ a combination of these techniques, ensuring that transactions are processed quickly, reliably, and correctly.

Concurrency control is an essential aspect of transaction processing, ensuring that transactions can execute concurrently without interfering with each other. Despite the complexity, effective concurrency control is one of the reasons mainframes continue to be trusted for handling critical, high-volume transaction processing workloads.

2.6 Transaction Recovery

TRANSACTION RECOVERY is a crucial aspect of any robust transaction processing system. Despite stringent measures, transactions can fail due to various reasons such as system failures, hardware malfunctions, network disruptions, or even data conflicts. When a failure occurs, the system must be able to recover to a consistent state without losing data. This section discusses how transaction processing systems achieve this.

2.6.1 The Need for Transaction Recovery

In the context of transaction processing, recovery means restoring the system to a consistent state after a transaction failure, ensuring that the ACID properties of transactions are maintained. Particularly, the principles of Atomicity and Durability come into play:

- Atomicity: If a transaction fails after partially executing, the changes it has made so far must be undone to maintain atomicity. This is known as rolling back the transaction.
- Durability: If a system failure occurs after a transaction has completed, the effects of the transaction must not be lost. This is achieved by preserving the changes in a durable medium and restoring them after the system recovers.

2.6.2 Recovery Techniques

Recovery from transaction failures is typically achieved through logging and checkpoints:

- Logging: A transaction log is maintained, recording the details of all transactions and their changes to the database.

The log allows the system to undo (rollback) or redo transactions as needed. There are two types of logs used:

- ○ Undo Log: This records the state of the data before the transaction, enabling the system to rollback a transaction by restoring the old data.
- ○ Redo Log: This records the changes made by the transaction, allowing the system to redo a transaction by applying these changes again.

- Checkpoints: A checkpoint is a point in the processing where the system writes all current changes in the log to the actual database. Checkpoints reduce the amount of processing needed for recovery by limiting the number of transactions that need to be undone or redone.

2.6.3 Recovery Process

The process of recovery involves two main steps: backward recovery (undo) and forward recovery (redo).

- Backward Recovery (Undo): This step undoes the effects of failed transactions. Starting from the most recent checkpoint, the system goes backwards through the log, undoing any uncommitted transactions it encounters.
- Forward Recovery (Redo): After all necessary transactions have been undone, the system goes forward through the log from the checkpoint, redoing any committed transactions that weren't reflected in the database due to the failure.

2.6.4 Transaction Recovery in Mainframes

Mainframes often process critical applications where even a small downtime can have significant consequences. Hence, they implement robust recovery mechanisms to minimize the impact of failures. Systems like IBM's CICS and DB2 provide comprehensive logging and checkpointing features, ensuring quick and accurate recovery from transaction failures.

In summary, transaction recovery is a vital aspect of transaction processing, ensuring the system's reliability and the integrity of data. Through techniques like logging and checkpointing, transaction processing systems can recover from failures, maintaining the ACID properties of transactions and ensuring smooth, uninterrupted operation.

2.7 Security in Transaction Processing

SECURITY IN TRANSACTION processing is of utmost importance as transactions often involve sensitive data and critical operations. Various security challenges can arise in transaction processing, ranging from unauthorized data access to data tampering. This section discusses the security challenges in transaction processing and the techniques used to mitigate them.

2.7.1 Security Challenges in Transaction Processing

Transaction processing faces several security challenges:

- Unauthorized Access: Unauthorized users may attempt to access or manipulate sensitive transaction data.
- Data Tampering: Even authorized users may attempt to tamper with transaction data for fraudulent purposes.
- Data Interception: During transmission, transaction data can be intercepted and misused.
- Denial of Service: Attackers may attempt to overload the transaction processing system, preventing legitimate users from processing transactions.

2.7.2 Security Measures in Transaction Processing

Various measures are used to address these security challenges:

- Encryption: Transaction data is often encrypted, both in storage and during transmission. This ensures that even if data is intercepted, it cannot be understood without the decryption key.
- Secure Protocols: Protocols like SSL/TLS are used for secure communication, providing features like encryption,

data integrity checks, and authentication.

- Authentication and Authorization: Users are required to authenticate (prove their identity) before accessing the system. Once authenticated, they are only authorized to perform certain actions based on their role.
- Access Control: Strict access control policies are implemented, defining who can access what data and what operations they can perform on it.
- Auditing: All transactions are logged, allowing any suspicious activity to be detected and investigated.

2.7.3 Security in Mainframe Transaction Processing

Mainframes, due to their use in processing critical transactions, have some of the most robust security measures in place. This includes hardware-level encryption, secure protocols for communication, sophisticated access control systems, and comprehensive auditing capabilities. IBM's Resource Access Control Facility (RACF) is an example of an advanced security system used in mainframes for managing access to resources.

2.7.4 Conclusion

Security in transaction processing is a vital aspect that cannot be overlooked. With proper security measures, businesses can ensure the confidentiality, integrity, and availability of their transaction data, maintaining trust with their customers and complying with regulations. As technology advances, security techniques continue to evolve, providing ever more robust protection against the ever-changing landscape of threats.

2.8 Role of Mainframes in Transaction Processing

MAINFRAMES HAVE LONG been at the heart of enterprise transaction processing. They are uniquely suited to handle high-volume, high-throughput, and high-availability workloads, which are characteristic of transaction processing systems. This section elaborates on the role of mainframes in transaction processing and the unique benefits they bring.

2.8.1 Performance and Scalability

One of the critical strengths of mainframes is their exceptional performance and scalability. Mainframes are designed to handle massive workloads reliably. They can support millions of transactions per second, making them an ideal choice for businesses that need to process large volumes of transactions daily. Moreover, they can be scaled up or out to accommodate growing workloads without a linear increase in cost or complexity.

2.8.2 Reliability and Availability

Mainframes are renowned for their reliability and availability. They feature redundant components and sophisticated error checking and recovery mechanisms that allow them to achieve near-zero downtime. This is essential for transaction processing systems, which often need to be available 24/7 and cannot afford to lose any transaction data due to a system failure.

2.8.3 Security

As discussed in the previous section, security is a paramount concern in transaction processing. Mainframes offer robust security features, including hardware-level encryption, secure communication protocols, and advanced access control systems. These features help ensure the confidentiality, integrity, and availability of transaction data.

2.8.4 Consolidation

Mainframes allow businesses to consolidate their workloads on a single system. This can greatly simplify the IT infrastructure, reducing complexity, overhead, and cost. It also allows for more efficient resource utilization, as resources can be dynamically allocated and shared among different workloads.

2.8.5 Conclusion

In conclusion, mainframes play a vital role in transaction processing. They provide the performance, reliability, security, and efficiency that transaction processing systems demand. Despite the emergence of new technologies and architectures, mainframes continue to be a trusted platform for mission-critical transaction processing. Their continuing relevance is testament to their unique strengths and the ongoing innovation in mainframe technology.

Chapter 3: Mainframes in the Modern World

3.1 Mainframes and Cloud Computing An in-depth look at how mainframes interact with and complement cloud computing architectures. This section covers the concept of "mainframe in the cloud," mainframe data virtualization, and the synergy between mainframes and cloud in terms of scalability, reliability, and cost-efficiency.

3.2 Mainframes and Big Data Discussing the significant role of mainframes in the era of big data. This part explains how mainframes contribute to big data processing, analytics, and data warehousing, and why they are instrumental in businesses' data strategies.

3.3 Mainframes and Microservices This section explores how modern software architectural patterns, like microservices, are being applied to mainframes to enhance modularity, agility, and continuous delivery. It discusses the integration of mainframes into DevOps pipelines and their role in modern application development.

3.4 Mainframes and Cybersecurity A deeper exploration of the security capabilities of mainframes, with a focus on the modern cybersecurity landscape. This part discusses how mainframes contribute to data security, compliance, and risk management in today's increasingly digital and interconnected world.

3.5 The Future of Mainframes Wrapping up the chapter by envisioning the future of mainframes. This part talks about the ongoing innovation in mainframe technology, the emerging trends

in mainframe usage, and the outlook for mainframes in the years to
come.

3.1 Mainframes and Cloud Computing

AS THE DIGITAL LANDSCAPE evolves, mainframes continue to adapt and find relevance. One of the significant shifts in recent years is the advent of cloud computing, which promises scalability, flexibility, and cost savings. This section explores how mainframes interact with and complement cloud computing architectures, creating a hybrid approach that leverages the strengths of both.

3.1.1 Mainframes in the Cloud

One of the emerging trends in the world of mainframes is the concept of "Mainframe as a Service" or "Mainframe in the Cloud". In this model, mainframe resources are made available on demand over the internet, similar to cloud services. It allows businesses to leverage the power of mainframes without needing to invest in and maintain their own mainframe infrastructure. Companies can scale up or down as needed, paying only for the resources they use.

This approach combines the advantages of mainframes (performance, reliability, security) with the advantages of cloud computing (scalability, flexibility, cost efficiency). Furthermore, it allows mainframe applications to seamlessly interact with cloud-native applications, facilitating digital transformation and modernization efforts.

3.1.2 Mainframe Data Virtualization

Another area where mainframes and cloud computing intersect is data virtualization. With the vast amounts of data processed and stored in mainframes, there's a growing need for modern, cloud-based applications to access this data. However, traditional data transfer methods are often slow, complex, and disruptive.

Mainframe data virtualization addresses this challenge. It provides a virtual view of the mainframe data, which can be accessed in real-time by cloud applications. This eliminates the need for data movement and replication, reducing latency and ensuring data consistency.

3.1.3 Synergy Between Mainframes and Cloud

Mainframes and cloud computing can work synergistically in several ways:

- Scalability: Cloud computing provides elastic scalability, allowing resources to be added or removed on demand. Mainframes, with their high throughput and performance, can handle the increased load when the system scales.
- Reliability: Mainframes are known for their reliability and near-zero downtime, which is critical for cloud services. They can provide a stable, dependable backbone for cloud infrastructures.
- Cost-Efficiency: Using mainframes in the cloud can be more cost-efficient than traditional mainframe ownership, as it reduces the need for upfront capital expenditure and ongoing maintenance costs.

3.1.4 Conclusion

In conclusion, the intersection of mainframes and cloud computing is an exciting space that is still evolving. By combining the strengths of mainframes and cloud, businesses can create robust, scalable, and efficient IT infrastructures that meet the demands of the modern digital world. The concept of mainframe in the cloud and mainframe data virtualization are two promising developments that are already showing their potential in various industries.

3.2 Mainframes and Big Data

AS WE TRANSITION INTO the era of big data, where massive amounts of data are generated and consumed every second, the relevance of mainframes is more pronounced than ever. This section discusses the significant role of mainframes in big data processing, analytics, and data warehousing, and why they are instrumental in businesses' data strategies.

3.2.1 Mainframes and Big Data Processing

Mainframes have the processing power to handle vast quantities of data in real-time. Their ability to perform millions of transactions per second allows them to process, sort, and analyze large data sets quickly and efficiently. This makes them ideally suited for big data processing, where speed and performance are of the essence.

Moreover, mainframes' ability to handle both structured and unstructured data allows them to work with various types of big data, from traditional databases to modern data types like social media posts, sensor data, and more.

3.2.2 Mainframes and Big Data Analytics

Data analytics is a core component of big data strategies, enabling businesses to extract valuable insights from their data. Mainframes provide a powerful platform for big data analytics, thanks to their processing power, storage capacity, and advanced analytics capabilities.

Mainframes can host and run sophisticated analytics tools and algorithms, allowing businesses to perform in-depth analysis on their data. They also support real-time analytics, which is crucial for applications like fraud detection, customer behavior analysis, and operational optimization.

3.2.3 Mainframes and Data Warehousing

Mainframes are also instrumental in data warehousing, which involves consolidating data from various sources into a single repository for analysis and reporting. The large storage capacity of mainframes, along with their robust data management capabilities, make them an excellent choice for hosting data warehouses.

Moreover, mainframes' data virtualization capabilities can streamline the data warehousing process. By providing a virtual view of the data, mainframes eliminate the need for data movement and replication, making it easier to integrate data from various sources and ensuring data consistency.

3.2.4 Mainframes in Business Data Strategies

Given their capabilities in big data processing, analytics, and data warehousing, mainframes are often at the heart of business data strategies. They provide a reliable, scalable, and efficient platform for managing and leveraging big data. Whether it's processing transactions, analyzing customer behavior, or generating business reports, mainframes play a critical role in turning data into actionable insights.

3.2.5 Conclusion

In the era of big data, mainframes continue to prove their worth. They bring power, performance, and reliability to big data initiatives, enabling businesses to make the most of their data. As the volume, variety, and velocity of data continue to grow, the role of mainframes in big data is likely to become even more significant.

3.3 Mainframes and Microservices

THE EMERGENCE OF MODERN architectural patterns like microservices has revolutionized software development, and mainframes have been no exception. This section explores how these patterns are being applied to mainframes to enhance modularity, agility, and continuous delivery. It also discusses the integration of mainframes into DevOps pipelines and their role in modern application development.

3.3.1 Microservices and Mainframes

Microservices architecture is a design pattern where an application is built as a suite of small, independent services that communicate over well-defined APIs. This architectural style brings several benefits, including modularity, scalability, and easier maintenance.

Applying this pattern to mainframes means breaking down monolithic mainframe applications into smaller, independent services. Each service can be developed, deployed, and scaled independently, increasing the agility of mainframe application development and making it easier to update or add new features.

3.3.2 Mainframes in the DevOps Pipeline

DevOps is a set of practices that combines software development and IT operations, aiming to shorten the system development life cycle and provide continuous delivery with high software quality. Mainframes, despite their traditional image, can fit well into DevOps pipelines.

By breaking mainframe applications into microservices, these services can be integrated into modern, automated CI/CD pipelines. Code can be built, tested, and deployed continuously, increasing the speed of delivery and improving the quality of software.

3.3.3 Mainframes and Modern Application Development

The integration of mainframes into modern development practices doesn't stop at microservices and DevOps. Mainframes can also work with modern programming languages, frameworks, and tools. For example, IBM Z mainframes can run applications written in Java, Python, and Node.js, among others.

Furthermore, mainframe data can be exposed through APIs, allowing it to be accessed by modern, cloud-native applications. This enables mainframes to participate in the broader ecosystem of modern application development, facilitating innovation and digital transformation.

3.3.4 Conclusion

In conclusion, the application of modern architectural patterns like microservices to mainframes is unlocking new potential in these powerful machines. By integrating mainframes into modern development practices like DevOps, businesses can enhance their agility, speed up their delivery, and leverage mainframes' power in new and innovative ways. The role of mainframes in modern application development is evolving, and it's exciting to imagine what the future holds.

3.4 Mainframes and Cybersecurity

IN AN ERA WHERE CYBERSECURITY threats are growing in number and sophistication, the security capabilities of mainframes are more vital than ever. This section takes a deeper exploration into these capabilities, with a focus on the modern cybersecurity landscape. It discusses how mainframes contribute to data security, compliance, and risk management in today's increasingly digital and interconnected world.

3.4.1 Mainframes and Data Security

Data security is a paramount concern for organizations, and mainframes excel in this regard. Mainframes are equipped with robust built-in security features designed to protect data from unauthorized access and attacks.

Encryption is a core component of mainframe data security. Modern mainframes offer pervasive encryption, meaning that all data can be encrypted, whether at rest or in transit, without requiring changes to applications or databases.

Access control is another vital aspect of mainframe security. Mainframes have sophisticated access control mechanisms that can enforce granular permissions, ensuring that only authorized users can access specific data.

3.4.2 Mainframes and Compliance

Regulatory compliance is a key concern for many industries, particularly those handling sensitive data like financial transactions, healthcare records, and personal data. Mainframes can greatly assist in meeting these regulatory requirements.

Mainframes' extensive logging and auditing capabilities make it easier to track and document actions, helping businesses prove their compliance with regulations like GDPR, HIPAA, PCI DSS, and more. Their robust security measures also help meet regulatory requirements around data protection and privacy.

3.4.3 Mainframes and Risk Management

From a risk management perspective, mainframes provide high availability and resilience, reducing the risk of downtime and data loss. They also offer features like redundant hardware, automatic failover, and disaster recovery capabilities, ensuring business continuity even in the face of hardware failures, natural disasters, or other disruptions.

Moreover, mainframes' strong security measures can help mitigate the risk of cyber attacks, data breaches, and other cybersecurity threats, protecting businesses from the potential financial and reputational damage these incidents can cause.

3.4.4 Mainframes in the Cybersecurity Landscape

In today's cybersecurity landscape, mainframes offer a unique combination of performance, reliability, and security. They provide a secure, dependable foundation for critical business operations, even as the volume and complexity of cybersecurity threats continue to grow.

However, it's essential to remember that mainframe security is not a "set it and forget it" proposition. It requires continuous monitoring, regular updates, and proactive measures to address emerging threats. This includes not only technological measures but also people and processes, like user education, security policies, and incident response plans.

3.4.5 Conclusion

In conclusion, mainframes play a vital role in cybersecurity, providing robust data security, facilitating regulatory compliance, and contributing to risk management. In an increasingly digital and interconnected world, their strengths in these areas are more important than ever. As we navigate the evolving cybersecurity landscape, the role of mainframes in protecting data and ensuring business continuity is likely to become even more significant.

3.5 The Future of Mainframes

AFTER TRAVERSING THROUGH the history, the present, and the many modern adaptations of mainframes, this section wraps up the chapter by envisioning the future of mainframes. It discusses the ongoing innovation in mainframe technology, the emerging trends in mainframe usage, and the outlook for mainframes in the years to come.

3.5.1 Ongoing Innovation in Mainframe Technology

Mainframe technology is continuously evolving. Innovations are underway in hardware performance, software capabilities, security, and integration with modern technologies. For instance, newer generations of mainframes are integrating AI capabilities, enhancing mainframe's data processing and analytical prowess. Innovations in quantum computing could also transform the capabilities of mainframes in the future.

3.5.2 Emerging Trends in Mainframe Usage

Trends in mainframe usage are being shaped by the ever-changing digital landscape. As businesses increasingly recognize the value of their mainframe data, they're seeking ways to leverage it in their digital transformation strategies. Hence, there's a growing trend towards opening up mainframes to modern application development and integrating them with cloud and big data architectures.

Moreover, as the world becomes more interconnected, mainframes are playing a critical role in the Internet of Things (IoT). Their ability to process massive volumes of transactions makes them ideal for managing the data generated by billions of IoT devices.

3.5.3 The Outlook for Mainframes

Looking forward, the future of mainframes appears bright. Despite the growth of newer technologies like cloud computing, mainframes continue to hold a crucial position in the world of IT due to their unmatched reliability, scalability, and security.

Furthermore, as we move into an era of big data and AI, the processing power of mainframes makes them increasingly relevant. They offer a robust platform for handling the vast amounts of data needed for machine learning and AI, and for providing real-time insights.

3.5.4 Conclusion

In conclusion, mainframes have a promising future. Ongoing innovation, emerging trends, and the evolving needs of the digital world are all pointing towards a continued role for mainframes in the years to come. While mainframes will undoubtedly continue to evolve, one thing is clear: these powerful machines are here to stay, and their influence in the digital world is set to grow.

Part II: Understanding Mainframe Transaction Processing

———

After exploring the fundamentals of mainframes and transaction processing, it's now time to delve deeper into the world of mainframe transaction processing. In Part II of this book, we explore the nuts and bolts of how mainframes handle transaction processing, discussing key topics like mainframe operating systems, mainframe databases, and transactional programming languages.

Chapter 4: Mainframe Operating Systems

The first chapter of this part takes you on a tour of mainframe operating systems, the software that runs on mainframes and manages their resources. We'll discuss the features and capabilities of popular mainframe operating systems, like z/OS, z/VM, and z/VSE, and how they handle transaction processing.

Chapter 5: Mainframe Databases and Transaction Processing

Next, we turn our attention to mainframe databases and their role in transaction processing. We explore different types of databases used in mainframes, like hierarchical, network, and relational databases, and discuss how they manage transactions. We also take a look at key database management systems for mainframes, such as DB2 and IMS.

Chapter 6: Mainframe Transactional Programming Languages

Finally, we delve into the world of mainframe programming languages, with a focus on those used for transaction processing. We discuss popular languages like COBOL, PL/I, and Java, exploring their features, syntax, and how they handle transactions on mainframes.

By the end of this part, you should have a solid understanding of how mainframes handle transaction processing, from the operating system to the database to the programming language. This knowledge will provide a solid foundation for the more advanced topics covered in Part III of the book.

Chapter 4: Mainframe Operating Systems

Mainframe operating systems are the engines that power mainframe computers, providing the framework that allows software applications to run and interact with hardware resources. This chapter focuses on these crucial elements of mainframes, discussing their key characteristics and how they handle transaction processing.

4.1 Introduction to Mainframe Operating Systems

In this section, we introduce the concept of mainframe operating systems, discussing their function and why they are so important for mainframes. We also provide a brief overview of the mainframe operating systems we will be exploring in this chapter.

4.2 z/OS

IBM's z/OS is the most widely used mainframe operating system. This section discusses the features and capabilities of z/OS, how it handles transaction processing, and why it is so popular.

4.3 z/VM

Another IBM operating system, z/VM is designed for mainframe virtualization. This part explains what z/VM is, its key features, and how it handles transactions.

4.4 z/VSE

z/VSE, or Virtual Storage Extended, is another mainframe operating system from IBM. This section explores the characteristics of z/VSE and its approach to transaction processing.

4.5 Linux on IBM Z

In this part, we discuss Linux on IBM Z, an adaptation of the open-source Linux operating system for IBM mainframes. We cover its features, benefits, and how it manages transactions.

4.6 Comparison of Mainframe Operating Systems

After exploring each operating system individually, this section compares them side by side, discussing their relative strengths and weaknesses, and which situations each one is best suited for.

4.7 Conclusion

The chapter concludes with a summary of the main points covered and a reflection on the importance of mainframe operating systems for transaction processing.

With this understanding of mainframe operating systems, we will be better equipped to explore mainframe databases and transactional programming languages in the following chapters.

4.1 Introduction to Mainframe Operating Systems

THE OPERATING SYSTEM (OS) is the backbone of any computer system, be it a personal computer or a high-end mainframe. In the context of mainframes, the OS takes on an even more critical role due to the scale and complexity of operations that mainframes handle.

A mainframe operating system is a software layer that manages the hardware resources of a mainframe computer and provides services for running applications. It handles important tasks such as managing memory, coordinating input and output (I/O) operations, and managing files and databases. More than that, a mainframe OS is specifically designed to support large-scale, high-volume processing and to provide extreme levels of reliability, security, and availability.

One of the key functions of a mainframe OS in the context of this book is handling transaction processing. In simple terms, a transaction is a sequence of operations that forms a single logical unit of work. For example, transferring money from one bank account to another involves several steps (checking the balance, debiting one account, crediting another, etc.), but from the user's perspective, it's a single transaction. The OS is responsible for ensuring that all these steps happen smoothly and reliably, and that either all of them succeed, or, in the case of an error, none of them affect the system's state.

In this chapter, we will explore several key mainframe operating systems that are commonly used for transaction processing:

- z/OS: IBM's flagship mainframe OS, known for its robustness, scalability, and advanced features for transaction processing.

- z/VM: An OS designed to provide virtualization capabilities on IBM Z mainframes.
- z/VSE: Another IBM mainframe OS, particularly suited for smaller mainframe installations and less complex workloads.
- Linux on IBM Z: An adaptation of the popular open-source Linux OS for IBM mainframes, offering the benefits of open-source development with the power of mainframe hardware.

Each of these operating systems offers its own unique features and benefits, and we'll dive into those in the sections to come.

4.2 z/OS

Z/OS IS IBM'S FLAGSHIP mainframe operating system, designed to provide the robustness, scalability, and performance necessary for mission-critical applications. Its primary characteristics lie in its support for symmetric multiprocessing, SMT (Simultaneous MultiThreading), high-volume input/output processing, strong security, and continuous availability.

One of the key features of z/OS is its support for both batch and online transaction processing. It offers a range of subsystems, such as Customer Information Control System (CICS), Information Management System (IMS), and DB2, which provide the foundation for building and running transactional applications.

CICS, for instance, is a powerful transaction processing system that supports high volumes of transactions. It's widely used in industries such as banking, insurance, and airline reservations, where large-scale, reliable transaction processing is essential.

Another essential aspect of z/OS is its security. With features like RACF (Resource Access Control Facility), z/OS provides comprehensive security management capabilities, ensuring secure transactions and protection of sensitive data. This is a fundamental requirement in many industries and is one of the reasons why z/OS is favored in environments where data security is paramount.

In addition, z/OS supports a range of languages, including COBOL, Java, C++, and others, making it a versatile platform for developing a wide variety of applications. It also provides exceptional support for IBM's DB2 database system, which is often used in conjunction with z/OS for handling complex, high-volume transaction processing.

Lastly, z/OS is renowned for its scalability and reliability. It's designed to handle huge workloads and provide near-continuous availability, making it a go-to choice for organizations that require round-the-clock operation and cannot afford downtime.

In short, z/OS's combination of robust transaction processing capabilities, strong security, support for multiple programming languages, and high reliability and scalability make it a leading choice for mainframe operating systems.

4.3 z/VM

Z/VM, OR Z/VIRTUAL Machine, is a mainframe operating system from IBM designed to provide virtualization capabilities on IBM's Z hardware platforms. It's built on IBM's earlier virtualization operating system, VM/370, and is known for its high performance, scalability, and security.

Virtualization, in the context of mainframes, refers to the ability to run multiple instances of operating systems concurrently on a single mainframe computer. Each instance, known as a virtual machine (VM), can run its own applications and workloads as though it were a separate physical machine. This allows mainframes to make more efficient use of their substantial computing resources and to provide a high degree of flexibility and isolation between workloads.

One of z/VM's key strengths is its support for a broad range of guest operating systems, including z/OS, z/VSE, Linux on IBM Z, and others. This makes it a versatile platform for running a diverse array of applications and workloads.

In terms of transaction processing, z/VM itself doesn't handle transactions in the way that z/OS does. Instead, transaction processing is typically handled by the guest operating systems and applications running on the virtual machines provided by z/VM. For instance, a z/OS instance running on z/VM would handle transactions using its own subsystems like CICS or IMS.

However, z/VM does provide crucial support for transaction processing in terms of resource management, scalability, and isolation. It ensures that each VM has the resources it needs to handle its workloads, can scale those resources up or down as necessary, and keeps the workloads isolated so that a problem in one VM doesn't affect others.

z/VM also includes robust security features, such as access controls, encryption capabilities, and audit logging, which help protect sensitive transaction data and ensure the integrity of the transaction processing environment.

In short, while z/VM isn't directly involved in transaction processing, it provides a flexible, scalable, and secure platform on which transaction processing systems can run.

4.4 z/VSE

Z/VSE, WHICH STANDS for Virtual Storage Extended, is a mainframe operating system developed by IBM primarily aimed at smaller mainframes and less complex workloads compared to z/OS. It's a reliable and cost-efficient solution for running dedicated applications, and despite its smaller scale focus, it does not compromise on the core attributes of reliability, security, and performance that mainframes are known for.

z/VSE supports the fundamental needs of transaction processing: reliable and secure data handling, high availability, and robust performance. However, it does so with an eye towards simplicity and cost-effectiveness that makes it a good fit for smaller businesses or specific use cases within larger organizations.

One of the key components for transaction processing in a z/VSE environment is the CICS Transaction Server. CICS provides an environment for running online transaction processing applications, enabling a high volume of transactions to be processed quickly and reliably. These applications can be written in various languages such as COBOL, PL/I, and C.

z/VSE also includes a database component, known as VSAM (Virtual Storage Access Method). VSAM is a file system and a database in one, used for storing and retrieving data in the context of transaction processing. It's known for its speed and efficiency, making it well suited to high-volume transaction workloads.

Security in z/VSE is handled by features like the Basic Security Manager (BSM), which provides user authentication and access control functionality. It ensures that only authorized users and programs can access sensitive transaction data.

z/VSE can also coexist with other operating systems in a virtualized environment under z/VM, making it a versatile option for organizations that need to run diverse workloads.

In summary, while z/VSE may not have all the features and capabilities of a larger-scale OS like z/OS, it's a reliable and efficient solution for transaction processing in smaller mainframe environments.

4.5 Linux on IBM Z

LINUX ON IBM Z, FORMERLY known as zLinux, is a version of the Linux operating system that's designed to run on IBM's Z series mainframes. By combining the flexibility and open-source advantages of Linux with the power and reliability of IBM's mainframe hardware, Linux on IBM Z provides a robust, scalable platform for running a wide variety of workloads, including transaction processing systems.

Linux on IBM Z supports all the standard features and capabilities of the Linux operating system, but with enhancements designed to take advantage of the mainframe's architecture. This includes features like hardware-assisted virtualization, dynamic resource allocation, and high-speed interprocess communication, all of which can contribute to the efficiency and performance of transaction processing systems.

For transaction processing, Linux on IBM Z can run a wide variety of open-source and commercial database systems and transaction processing monitors. Examples include MySQL, PostgreSQL, and Oracle for databases, and JBoss, WebSphere, and even CICS Transaction Gateway for transaction processing. This gives businesses a great deal of flexibility in choosing the software stack that best meets their needs.

Linux on IBM Z also offers the advantage of being fully integrated with the larger ecosystem of Linux software. This means businesses can leverage a broad range of tools and applications that are familiar to many developers and system administrators. Furthermore, being part of the open-source community, Linux on IBM Z benefits from the community's innovations and continuous improvements.

On the security front, Linux on IBM Z leverages the mainframe's built-in security features, such as hardware-assisted encryption and secure key management, while also supporting the full range of security features available in the Linux environment. This can help ensure that transaction data is protected both at rest and in transit.

In summary, Linux on IBM Z provides a flexible, powerful platform for transaction processing, combining the strengths of the Linux ecosystem with the performance and reliability of IBM's mainframe hardware.

4.6 Comparison of Mainframe Operating Systems

CHOOSING THE RIGHT operating system for your mainframe largely depends on your business needs, the nature of your workloads, and the skills and expertise of your IT team. Let's compare the operating systems discussed in this chapter to give you a better understanding of how they stack up against each other.

z/OS

z/OS is the flagship operating system for IBM mainframes, known for its robustness, reliability, and scalability. It's designed to handle massive workloads and high volumes of transactions, making it ideal for large enterprises in sectors like banking, insurance, and retail, where high performance and continuous availability are paramount.

Key features of z/OS include support for multiple programming languages, sophisticated resource management, advanced security features, and built-in support for transaction processing through subsystems like CICS and IMS. However, z/OS can be complex to manage and require specialized skills, which might be a consideration for some organizations.

z/VM

z/VM is a mainframe operating system focused on virtualization. It allows running multiple instances of various operating systems concurrently on a single mainframe machine. This flexibility makes it a good choice for organizations that need to run diverse workloads or want to make the most efficient use of their mainframe resources.

While z/VM doesn't handle transaction processing directly, it provides a robust, scalable, and secure environment in which transaction processing systems can run. However, managing a virtualized environment can be complex, and like z/OS, z/VM requires specialized skills.

z/VSE

z/VSE is a smaller-scale mainframe operating system that's designed to be simple and cost-effective. It's a good fit for smaller businesses or for specific use cases within larger organizations that don't require the full range of capabilities provided by z/OS.

z/VSE supports transaction processing through the CICS Transaction Server and the VSAM database system. Its smaller scale and simplicity can make it easier to manage than z/OS or z/VM, but it may not be as suitable for very large or complex workloads.

Linux on IBM Z

Linux on IBM Z combines the open-source flexibility of Linux with the power of IBM mainframes. This makes it a highly versatile option that can run a wide variety of workloads, including transaction processing.

Linux on IBM Z supports a wide range of open-source and commercial database and transaction processing systems. It also benefits from the innovations and continuous improvements of the open-source community. The familiar Linux environment may be easier for some teams to work with, but it might not offer the same level of integration with mainframe hardware and software features as the other IBM operating systems.

In conclusion, each of these operating systems has its strengths and is suited to different situations. The best choice depends on your specific needs and circumstances.

4.7 Conclusion

THIS CHAPTER HAS TAKEN you on a journey through the world of mainframe operating systems, each with its unique strengths and features, designed to address specific use cases. It started with an overview of what mainframe operating systems are and their crucial role in managing the efficient and secure execution of tasks on mainframes.

We then delved into the specifics of four significant mainframe operating systems: IBM's z/OS, z/VM, and z/VSE, along with Linux on IBM Z. The exploration of each system gave insights into its unique capabilities, transaction processing abilities, and where it fits in the diverse world of business computing needs.

Our comparison of these operating systems highlighted their relative strengths and weaknesses, providing you with a clearer understanding of their unique value propositions. It underscored that the best choice of operating system depends significantly on the nature of the workload, business needs, the organization's resources, and technical expertise.

As we have seen, mainframe operating systems are the beating heart of the mainframe, enabling it to perform its powerful data processing and transaction handling capabilities. They provide the infrastructure necessary for running high-volume, high-speed transaction processing applications, playing a vital role in ensuring efficiency, security, and reliability.

As we move forward, keep in mind that the choice of operating system is a fundamental decision that can significantly impact the performance and capabilities of your mainframe transaction processing system. The more you understand about these operating systems, the better equipped you'll be to make the right choice for your organization.

In the next chapters, we will be moving deeper into the world of mainframe transaction processing, discussing mainframe databases, and transactional programming languages, helping you understand the technicalities involved in managing and executing transactions on mainframes.

Chapter 5: Mainframe Databases and Transaction Processing

5.1 Introduction to Mainframe Databases This section provides an overview of mainframe databases, explaining their role, characteristics, and significance in the context of mainframes and transaction processing.

5.2 Hierarchical Databases: IBM Information Management System (IMS) IMS, a type of hierarchical database, is discussed in detail in this section. It covers the architecture, features, and transaction processing capabilities of IMS.

5.3 Relational Databases: DB2 This part explores IBM's DB2, a widely-used relational database system on mainframes. It provides an understanding of its structure, functions, and how it facilitates transaction processing.

5.4 Navigational Databases: IDMS An exploration of IDMS, a navigational database system used on mainframes. This section explains how IDMS is designed, how it works, and its role in transaction processing.

5.5 Comparison of Mainframe Databases After covering each database type, this section compares them, highlighting their respective strengths and weaknesses, and discussing which scenarios they are best suited for.

5.6 Mainframe Databases and Transaction Management Here we delve into how mainframe databases manage transactions, looking at the various techniques used to ensure data consistency, integrity, and recoverability.

5.7 Modern Developments: NoSQL and Mainframes This part examines the emergence of NoSQL databases on mainframes, discussing what NoSQL is, its benefits, and how it interacts with transaction processing on mainframes.

5.8 Conclusion The chapter concludes with a summary of the key points covered, and a reflection on the importance of understanding mainframe databases for effective transaction processing.

5.1 Introduction to Mainframe Databases

IN THE DIGITAL AGE, data is one of the most valuable resources, and databases are the heart of data management, storage, and retrieval. As the name suggests, mainframe databases are databases that are hosted on mainframes, managing vast volumes of data and offering high-speed, secure, and reliable data processing capabilities. They play an integral role in industries where large-scale transaction processing is critical, such as banking, healthcare, and retail.

Mainframe databases are specifically designed to handle the unique requirements of mainframe environments, including handling high transaction volumes, providing continuous availability, ensuring data consistency, and maintaining stringent security standards. Their design enables them to handle numerous concurrent transactions and provide quick response times, even under heavy loads.

Furthermore, mainframe databases offer a robust recovery mechanism, ensuring that the database can recover quickly and correctly from any failures, thus minimizing downtime and data loss. They also ensure the ACID (Atomicity, Consistency, Isolation, Durability) properties of transactions, which is fundamental for preserving data integrity and consistency.

Mainframe databases are of various types, each with its own strengths and characteristics. The most common types include hierarchical databases (such as IBM's Information Management System, or IMS), relational databases (such as IBM's DB2), and navigational databases (such as IDMS). More recently, NoSQL databases have also started making their way into the mainframe world, offering flexibility and scalability to handle diverse data types and structures.

In the subsequent sections of this chapter, we will delve deeper into these different types of mainframe databases, their architecture, features, and how they handle transaction processing. Understanding these databases is vital because they are the backbone of mainframe transaction processing, playing a critical role in ensuring that transactions are processed quickly, accurately, and securely.

5.2 Hierarchical Databases: IBM Information Management System (IMS)

IBM'S INFORMATION MANAGEMENT System (IMS) is one of the oldest and most robust mainframe database systems. Introduced in the 1960s, it is a type of hierarchical database management system that has stood the test of time due to its robustness, reliability, and exceptional processing speeds.

The hierarchical nature of IMS refers to its data structure, where data is organized in a tree-like model. This model comprises nodes representing records and branches representing fields or relationships. The topmost node is called the root, and the lines connecting nodes are known as paths. This structure mirrors real-world relationships well and allows efficient data access.

One of IMS's key strengths is its performance. Its hierarchical model, coupled with its mainframe hosting environment, enables IMS to handle incredibly high volumes of transactions with remarkable speed and efficiency. Industries with high transaction volumes, such as banking and airlines, have therefore heavily relied on IMS over the years.

In addition to its data management capabilities, IMS also includes a transaction manager component: IMS Transaction Manager (IMS TM). IMS TM plays a crucial role in coordinating and managing transactions, ensuring their atomicity, consistency, and durability. It also manages system resources, schedules tasks, and controls concurrency to ensure that transactions do not interfere with each other.

Despite its age, IMS remains highly relevant in the modern digital era, thanks to continual updates and enhancements from IBM.

These updates have included improved support for web-based interfaces, integration capabilities with other databases and systems, and enhanced security features, ensuring that IMS can meet today's transaction processing demands.

In essence, IMS's longevity, robustness, and performance make it a cornerstone of mainframe transaction processing, offering unparalleled efficiency and reliability for high-volume transaction processing tasks.

5.3 Relational Databases: DB2

IBM'S DB2 IS A RELATIONAL database management system (RDBMS) specifically designed for mainframe environments. Introduced in the 1980s, DB2 has become one of the most popular databases for mainframe transaction processing, thanks to its powerful features, scalability, and reliability.

Relational databases like DB2 differ from hierarchical databases like IMS in the way they organize data. In a relational model, data is stored in tables composed of rows and columns. Each row represents a unique record, and each column represents a field of the record. This structure allows for greater flexibility and simplicity in data management, as data from different tables can be linked or joined based on common values, or keys.

DB2 boasts many strengths that make it ideal for transaction processing. It can handle vast amounts of data and high transaction loads, offering excellent performance and speed. Its support for SQL (Structured Query Language) allows for complex data queries and manipulations. It also includes robust security features, including access controls, auditing capabilities, and encryption, ensuring that transactions and data are secure.

DB2's ACID compliance is central to its transaction management capabilities. It ensures the Atomicity, Consistency, Isolation, and Durability of each transaction, maintaining data integrity and consistency even in the face of system failures or concurrent transactions.

DB2 also offers features to enhance performance and usability. These include support for XML data, machine learning capabilities, and integration with big data platforms like Hadoop. It also provides utilities for database administration, including tools for backup and recovery, performance tuning, and data replication.

As with IMS, DB2 has continued to evolve, with IBM regularly releasing updates to enhance its capabilities and ensure it remains at the cutting edge of database technology. Its combination of power, flexibility, and continual improvement makes DB2 an essential tool in the mainframe transaction processing toolkit.

5.4 Navigational Databases: IDMS

INTEGRATED DATABASE Management System (IDMS) is a navigational database management system developed originally by B.F. Goodrich and later acquired by Computer Associates (now known as CA Technologies). It is renowned for its ability to manage and process complex networks of data with exceptional efficiency and reliability on mainframes.

Navigational databases, such as IDMS, organize data as sets or records, similar to a hierarchical database but with added flexibility. While hierarchical databases strictly enforce a tree-like structure, navigational databases allow for more complex relationships. In IDMS, records (similar to rows in a relational database) are connected via sets, enabling a record to be a member of multiple sets and establishing a network-like structure.

IDMS is particularly well-suited to transaction processing in environments where relationships between data items are complex and numerous. Its navigational data model enables efficient and rapid navigation through these relationships, providing quick data access during transactions.

One of the core features of IDMS is its strong transaction management capabilities. Its transaction processing subsystem ensures the ACID (Atomicity, Consistency, Isolation, Durability) properties of transactions, allowing for concurrent transaction processing while maintaining data integrity and consistency.

IDMS also provides extensive data recovery mechanisms and robust security features, further cementing its reliability in transaction processing. Its recoverability ensures that in the event of a failure, all completed transactions remain intact and any incomplete transactions are rolled back to maintain consistency. Its security features help protect sensitive data from unauthorized access.

Over the years, IDMS has been continually updated and enhanced to remain competitive in the evolving mainframe environment. Today, IDMS continues to serve many organizations that require efficient handling of complex data relationships and high-volume transaction processing.

5.5 Comparison of Mainframe Databases

HAVING EXPLORED VARIOUS mainframe database systems, it is valuable to draw comparisons and consider their unique strengths and potential applications. The three primary types we've discussed are hierarchical (IMS), relational (DB2), and navigational (IDMS) databases.

Hierarchical Databases: IMS

- Strengths: IMS shines with its excellent performance and efficiency in environments where data relationships are hierarchical. Its transaction processing capabilities are robust, and it excels at handling high-volume transactions, which makes it suitable for applications such as airline reservations or banking systems.
- Weaknesses: However, the hierarchical model's rigidity can make it less flexible when data relationships are complex and non-hierarchical.

Relational Databases: DB2

- Strengths: DB2, as a relational database, is incredibly flexible due to its table-based structure. It can manage complex data relationships with relative ease and is highly scalable, making it ideal for large enterprises dealing with a variety of applications. DB2's support for SQL, a ubiquitous data querying language, adds to its versatility.
- Weaknesses: While DB2 handles complex relationships well, it might require more resources than a hierarchical or navigational database for certain tasks, such as traversing deeply nested hierarchical data.

Navigational Databases: IDMS

- Strengths: IDMS is particularly effective when data relationships are complex and multi-directional. Its navigational data model facilitates rapid and efficient navigation through interconnected data sets. It also offers strong transaction management capabilities, making it ideal for high-volume transaction processing where data relationships are multifaceted.
- Weaknesses: However, IDMS may require more complex programming to manipulate and query data compared to relational databases.

In terms of transaction processing, all three databases offer robust features that ensure the ACID properties of transactions, although the specifics of their implementation vary. All have strong data recovery and security mechanisms, crucial for any transaction processing system.

The choice between these database systems often depends on the specific requirements of the application and environment. It's not about which database system is "better," but rather which one is most suited to a particular use case. A comprehensive understanding of each system can guide that crucial decision, ensuring efficiency and effectiveness in mainframe transaction processing.

5.6 Mainframe Databases and Transaction Management

MAINFRAME DATABASES have intricate transaction management mechanisms to ensure the ACID properties (Atomicity, Consistency, Isolation, Durability) of transactions. These mechanisms ensure that transactions complete successfully or, in case of failure, the system reverts back to its original state without causing inconsistency or data loss. Let's delve into how these databases manage transactions.

Atomicity: The principle of atomicity ensures that a transaction is treated as a single, indivisible unit of work. It stipulates that all operations within a transaction must complete successfully for the transaction to be considered successful. If any part of the transaction fails, the entire transaction is rolled back, ensuring the database remains in a consistent state. Mainframe databases employ sophisticated transaction control mechanisms, like rollback and rollforward operations, to guarantee atomicity.

Consistency: Consistency ensures that a transaction brings the database from one valid state to another, maintaining the integrity of the database. Mainframe databases utilize integrity constraints and consistency rules that must be adhered to by each transaction. These rules are checked before a transaction is committed. If a transaction violates these rules, it is rolled back to ensure the database remains consistent.

Isolation: Isolation ensures that concurrent transactions do not interfere with each other. Mainframe databases implement isolation using concurrency control mechanisms such as locking, latching, and versioning. These techniques prevent conflicts that can arise from multiple transactions attempting to modify the same data simultaneously.

Durability: Durability guarantees that once a transaction is committed, its changes to the database are permanent and survive any subsequent system failures. Mainframe databases achieve durability using various methods, including transaction logging, checkpointing, and backup procedures. Transaction logs record all changes made by a transaction, enabling recovery if a failure occurs. Checkpointing is a process that periodically saves the state of a transaction to persistent storage, reducing the amount of work needed for recovery.

These principles collectively ensure that mainframe databases can handle a high volume of transactions with efficiency, reliability, and robustness. They make these systems ideally suited to industries such as banking, healthcare, and retail, where processing high volumes of transactions accurately and quickly is of utmost importance.

5.7 Modern Developments: NoSQL and Mainframes

NOSQL DATABASES HAVE gained popularity in the modern software landscape due to their scalability, flexibility, and performance benefits. More recently, the power of NoSQL is being harnessed in the world of mainframes to meet the evolving needs of data storage and transaction processing.

NoSQL, which stands for "Not Only SQL," refers to a group of databases that provide a way of storing and retrieving data that is modeled differently than the traditional relational databases. These databases are especially useful when dealing with large volumes of structured, semi-structured, or unstructured data. They are designed for distributed data stores where very large scale and availability are requirements.

There are four main types of NoSQL databases: key-value stores, document databases, wide-column stores, and graph databases. Each of these has its unique strengths, and the choice of database depends on the specific requirements of the application.

In the context of mainframes, NoSQL databases are increasingly being used to manage the vast amount of data generated by today's digital businesses. They complement existing mainframe databases like DB2 and IMS by providing capabilities that are more suited to certain types of workloads.

For transaction processing, NoSQL databases offer a few key benefits. First, they can handle high-velocity, high-volume data. In today's digital world, transactions are not limited to financial operations. Every interaction, from clicks on a website to sensor readings in an IoT device, can be a transaction. NoSQL databases can handle these large volumes of data and provide near-real-time processing capabilities.

Second, NoSQL databases can handle a variety of data types. Traditional transactions typically involve structured data. However, modern transactions can include a mix of structured, semi-structured, and unstructured data. NoSQL databases are built to handle this data variety.

Finally, NoSQL databases offer a flexible schema. This allows businesses to adapt quickly to changes in data requirements, a common occurrence in today's fast-paced digital environments.

To leverage these benefits, mainframe systems now incorporate NoSQL databases in their data management architectures. This ensures that mainframes continue to deliver high performance, reliability, and scalability while meeting the modern requirements of transaction processing.

5.8 Conclusion

MAINFRAME DATABASES are a cornerstone of transaction processing, enabling businesses to store, retrieve, and manage data with efficiency, reliability, and security. Over the course of this chapter, we have explored various types of mainframe databases, including hierarchical databases like IMS, relational databases like DB2, navigational databases like IDMS, and emerging NoSQL databases.

Each type of database brings its unique strengths to the table. IMS and IDMS provide deep-rooted structures and reliable transactional capabilities that are well-suited for specific industry applications. DB2, being a relational database, offers a robust platform for managing structured data and complex transactions. NoSQL databases, on the other hand, cater to the modern needs of handling large volumes of varied data, providing scalability and flexibility that are instrumental in today's digital business environments.

Understanding these databases and their transaction management capabilities is crucial to leveraging the power of mainframes in today's world. As we move further into the digital age, mainframes and their databases continue to evolve, offering enhanced functionalities to meet the emerging needs of businesses.

The next time you engage with a mainframe transaction, whether it be making a bank transfer, booking a flight, or just browsing an online catalog, remember the complex orchestration of databases and transaction processing techniques working seamlessly behind the scenes to provide you with a smooth experience. The beauty of mainframes lies in their unwavering reliability, immense scalability, and intricate yet efficient transaction processing systems. As we continue to innovate and push technological boundaries, mainframes remain an integral part of our digital journey, proving time and again that they are far from being obsolete.

Chapter 6: Mainframe Transactional Programming Languages

6.1 Introduction to Mainframe Transactional Programming Languages An introduction to the programming languages used in mainframe transaction processing. This section discusses their role, features, and significance.

6.2 COBOL (Common Business-Oriented Language) An in-depth look at COBOL, one of the oldest and most widely used mainframe programming languages. We discuss its syntax, structure, and how it handles transactions.

6.3 Java on Mainframes This part explores how Java, a popular, versatile, and platform-independent language, is used in mainframe transaction processing.

6.4 PL/I (Programming Language One) An exploration of PL/I, a powerful language designed for scientific, engineering, and business applications on mainframes.

6.5 CICS (Customer Information Control System) This section focuses on CICS, a transaction server that supports the rapid, high-volume, online transaction processing capabilities of mainframes.

6.6 Assembler An overview of Assembler, a low-level programming language commonly used on mainframes for tasks that require a high degree of control over system resources.

6.7 Emerging Languages: Python and Swift on Mainframes This part discusses the advent of modern programming languages, like Python and Swift, in the mainframe environment.

6.8 Conclusion A summary and conclusion of the chapter, reflecting on the importance of programming languages in mainframe transaction processing.

6.1 Introduction to Mainframe Transactional Programming Languages

MAINFRAME TRANSACTION processing is a complex orchestration of numerous components, with programming languages serving as the crucial conduits that enable effective communication between these components. These languages allow developers to write programs that interact with the mainframe's operating system, databases, and transaction processing systems to carry out various business operations.

Different programming languages are used on mainframes, each with its unique characteristics, advantages, and use cases. Some languages have been specifically designed for mainframes, while others, originally developed for different environments, have been adapted for use on mainframes due to their versatility and powerful capabilities.

Mainframe programming languages play a significant role in transaction processing. They provide the constructs necessary to define, manage, and control transactions, ensuring data integrity, security, and consistency. Moreover, they enable the development of business applications capable of processing a high volume of transactions efficiently and reliably.

In this chapter, we will delve into some of the most commonly used mainframe programming languages, including COBOL, Java, PL/I, CICS, and Assembler. We will also explore the emergence of modern languages such as Python and Swift in the mainframe environment. Understanding these languages, their capabilities, and how they facilitate transaction processing is key to fully harnessing the power of mainframes. Whether you are a seasoned mainframe professional looking to deepen your knowledge, or a newcomer eager to learn the ropes, this chapter will provide valuable insights into the fascinating world of mainframe transactional programming languages.

6.2 COBOL (Common Business-Oriented Language)

INTRODUCED IN THE LATE 1950s, COBOL (Common Business-Oriented Language) is one of the oldest programming languages still in use today. It was designed with business data processing in mind, with an emphasis on readability and ease of use. As a result, COBOL code often resembles natural English language, which is one of its distinctive features.

COBOL's structure consists of four divisions: Identification, Environment, Data, and Procedure. The Identification Division specifies the name and type of the program. The Environment Division describes the computer environment where the program will run. The Data Division is where all the data items processed by the program are defined, and the Procedure Division contains the actual code that manipulates data.

In transaction processing, COBOL plays a crucial role. Its file handling capabilities, built-in arithmetic operations, and strong data typing make it particularly suitable for writing applications that handle a large number of transactions.

COBOL can interface with popular transaction processing monitors like IBM's CICS (Customer Information Control System) or IMS (Information Management System), enabling the development of interactive applications capable of handling high-volume, online transactions. These applications can perform a variety of operations such as updating account balances, processing orders, or managing inventory, all in real-time and with a high degree of reliability.

Furthermore, COBOL's record-locking capabilities facilitate concurrent transaction processing. When multiple transactions try to access the same data, COBOL ensures that only one transaction can update the data at a time, preventing data inconsistency and corruption.

Despite its age, COBOL remains relevant and widely used in mainframe environments. The language's robustness, reliability, and unparalleled performance in high-volume transaction processing make it an enduring choice for many businesses, particularly in the financial and governmental sectors where mainframes dominate.

6.3 Java on Mainframes

ORIGINALLY DESIGNED by Sun Microsystems in the 1990s, Java has since become one of the most popular programming languages in the world. Its core mantra, "write once, run anywhere," reflects its design goal: platform independence. This means that a Java program can theoretically run on any device capable of running a Java Virtual Machine (JVM).

Java's widespread adoption didn't skip over mainframes. Today, Java is extensively used in mainframe environments due to its robust feature set, object-oriented design, built-in security measures, and its capacity to handle large-scale, complex applications.

One of the key advantages of using Java on mainframes is the ability to leverage existing infrastructure and data. Java applications running on the mainframe have direct, high-speed access to critical data residing on the mainframe, leading to increased efficiency and performance.

In the context of transaction processing, Java offers significant benefits. The language's concurrency utilities, including threads and locks, allow efficient handling of simultaneous transactions. Java also supports distributed transactions, enabling a single transaction to span multiple databases or data sources. Moreover, Java integrates well with transaction processing monitors like CICS and IMS, further enhancing its transaction management capabilities.

Java's exception handling mechanisms also play a vital role in transaction processing. If a problem occurs during a transaction, an exception is thrown, allowing the system to catch and handle the error without crashing the entire application. This ensures that transactions are either fully completed or entirely rolled back, preserving the integrity of the data.

Another advantage is the vast ecosystem of Java libraries and frameworks that can be used to simplify and expedite the development of transaction processing applications. Frameworks like Spring, Hibernate, and Jakarta EE (formerly Java EE) provide ready-made solutions for many common programming challenges, including transaction management.

In summary, Java brings modern, object-oriented programming to the mainframe, bridging the gap between legacy systems and current technological needs. Its versatility, performance, and integrative capabilities make it a powerful tool for mainframe transaction processing.

6.4 PL/I (Programming Language One)

PROGRAMMING LANGUAGE One, or PL/I, is a comprehensive, multipurpose programming language designed for both scientific and business applications. Developed by IBM in the 1960s, it was intended to replace both FORTRAN for scientific computation and COBOL for business data processing, uniting the two worlds under a single, powerful language.

PL/I was engineered to take advantage of the capabilities of mainframes, and it integrates well with mainframe systems and environments. The language is robust and highly flexible, supporting a variety of programming paradigms including imperative, procedural, and data-oriented models. It also provides extensive error checking and debugging capabilities, making it a reliable choice for mainframe programming.

In the realm of transaction processing, PL/I offers valuable features. Like COBOL, PL/I has robust file handling capabilities, a crucial feature for transaction processing systems. PL/I's built-in record I/O capabilities make it well suited for handling structured data and direct access files.

PL/I also supports concurrency and multitasking. Using PL/I's tasking capabilities, programmers can write applications where multiple tasks proceed in parallel, which is vital in high-volume transaction processing. These concurrent tasks can communicate and synchronize through PL/I's built-in inter-task communication mechanisms.

The language has exception handling mechanisms, too, allowing for the detection and handling of errors during the execution of a transaction. This ensures that a single failing transaction does not bring down the entire system and that failed transactions can be appropriately rolled back or retried.

Despite being an older language, PL/I continues to be used on mainframes today, particularly in environments that require a blend of computational power and business-oriented data processing. While not as popular or widely used as COBOL or Java, PL/I remains a powerful tool in the arsenal of mainframe programming languages, especially in the domain of transaction processing.

6.5 CICS (Customer Information Control System)

THE CUSTOMER INFORMATION Control System, better known as CICS, is a transaction server that was developed by IBM for mainframe systems. It is one of the most extensively used mainframe software for transaction processing. Its purpose is to provide a robust and high-performance environment for running and managing business applications.

CICS provides a multitasking environment where each business transaction is processed as a separate task. This is of particular importance in situations where a high volume of transactions are being processed concurrently, which is often the case with mainframes.

CICS supports a variety of programming languages including COBOL, Java, PL/I, and C++. This provides programmers with flexibility in choosing the language they are most comfortable with or that is most suited to the specific task at hand.

In the context of transaction processing, CICS plays a vital role. It supports the ACID properties (Atomicity, Consistency, Isolation, and Durability) that are crucial for reliable transaction processing. CICS handles the management of these properties, allowing developers to focus on business logic rather than low-level transaction management.

Atomicity ensures that a transaction is treated as a single unit of work, and that either all changes are committed to the database, or none are. Consistency guarantees that transactions bring the system from one consistent state to another. Isolation ensures that concurrent execution of transactions leaves the system in the same state that would have been obtained if the transactions were executed sequentially. Durability guarantees that once a transaction has been committed, it will remain committed even in the case of subsequent failures.

CICS also includes error recovery routines and security checks that are important for ensuring the smooth and secure operation of transaction processing systems.

CICS has undergone continuous development and enhancements over the years, with features added to support web interfaces, E-business operations, and integration with other software like DB2 and IMS.

To summarize, CICS forms an integral part of many mainframe transaction processing environments, offering features and capabilities that enhance the robustness, reliability, and efficiency of these systems.

6.6 Assembler

ASSEMBLER IS A LOW-level programming language that is closely associated with the hardware architecture of the system it is written for. Each assembly language is specific to a particular computer architecture, in contrast to high-level languages like Java or COBOL, which are generally portable across multiple systems.

In the context of mainframes, Assembler (often referred to as "IBM Assembler" or "HLASM" for High-Level Assembler) is commonly used for tasks that require a high degree of control over system resources or when maximum performance is necessary.

An Assembler program allows a programmer to use mnemonic representations of machine instructions, which makes the code easier to read and write than using raw machine code. However, compared to high-level languages, Assembler is much more complex and harder to master, due to its low-level nature and the need to manage system resources manually.

Despite the complexity, Assembler provides several benefits. Since it is a low-level language, it allows programs to be extremely efficient and fast. It also provides direct hardware control, allowing programmers to optimize their code for the specific architecture of the mainframe.

In transaction processing, Assembler can be used to write highly optimized routines that can handle critical tasks or performance-sensitive parts of the system. However, its use is typically limited to these specific scenarios due to the greater difficulty in writing and maintaining Assembler code compared to high-level languages.

While Assembler is less commonly used today for writing entire applications, it is often used for creating system software, such as operating systems and compilers. Additionally, understanding Assembler can provide valuable insight into how the computer works at a fundamental level, making it an important area of study for those seeking a deep understanding of mainframes.

6.7 Emerging Languages: Python and Swift on Mainframes

AS THE MAINFRAME CONTINUES to evolve, it has embraced modern programming languages to stay relevant and accessible to today's generation of developers. Two such languages that have gained popularity in the mainframe environment are Python and Swift.

Python on Mainframes

Python, known for its simplicity and readability, has been welcomed by the mainframe community. Python's versatility allows it to perform a variety of tasks such as automating tasks, creating web services, and even working with databases. As such, it can be used in conjunction with traditional mainframe languages for transaction processing, data manipulation, and more.

For instance, Python's z/OS modules allow developers to interact with z/OS system services, enabling integration with traditional mainframe workloads. This means Python scripts can be used to automate tasks, manipulate data, and interact with transaction processing systems, among other things.

Swift on Mainframes

Swift, created by Apple and open-sourced in 2015, has also found its way to the mainframe. Swift's focus on safety, speed, and expressivity has made it a favorite among developers, and its compatibility with IBM's LinuxONE and Linux on Z systems has made it a viable option for mainframe application development.

Although Swift is primarily used for developing iOS apps, its efficiency and ease of use make it an appealing choice for backend development on mainframes as well. The introduction of Swift on mainframes showcases the ongoing efforts to modernize mainframe development and make it more accessible to today's developers.

The inclusion of these contemporary languages highlights the mainframe's continued evolution. By supporting these languages, mainframes become more attractive to a broader base of developers, ensuring their continued relevance in the modern computing landscape. These languages also provide new methods for handling and processing transactions, supplementing the capabilities provided by traditional mainframe languages.

6.8 Conclusion

IN THE BROAD SPECTRUM of mainframe transaction processing, programming languages are fundamental. They dictate how transactions are defined, processed, and managed. From the seasoned languages like COBOL and PL/I that have stood the test of time, to the transaction server capabilities of CICS, to the low-level control offered by Assembler, and finally to the modern versatility of languages like Java, Python, and Swift - each language has its unique strengths and application domains.

COBOL's enduring popularity is a testament to its robustness and suitability for business applications, particularly in transaction processing. The adoption of Java on mainframes demonstrated the platform's capacity for evolution, with the ability to support object-oriented programming and integration with web technologies. Python and Swift represent the latest step in this evolutionary journey, bringing the simplicity and flexibility of modern languages to the world of mainframes.

The diversity of languages available for mainframe programming ensures that developers can choose the most suitable tool for the task at hand, whether that involves managing complex transactions, manipulating data, or integrating with other systems.

The important takeaway is that mainframes, often perceived as relics of the past, are not only relevant but are continuously adapting to the present and future of technology. This dynamism is reflected in the variety of programming languages they support, each contributing to the effectiveness and efficiency of mainframe transaction processing in its own unique way.

As we continue to navigate the ever-evolving landscape of technology, it is crucial to understand these programming languages' roles in leveraging mainframe technology. In the end, it is through these languages that we can truly tap into the power of mainframes and continue to drive innovation in transaction processing.

Part III: Detailed Aspects of Mainframe Transaction Processing

---

In this part of the book, we delve deeper into the world of mainframe transaction processing. We will focus on the intricate aspects and detailed workings of key systems, languages, and processes associated with mainframe transaction processing. The objective of this part is to provide a profound understanding of how transaction processing works on mainframes and why it remains an essential aspect of many modern businesses and industries.

Chapter 7: Understanding CICS - Customer Information Control System This chapter provides an in-depth understanding of the Customer Information Control System (CICS), a transaction server that powers billions of transactions every day. We will explore its architecture, components, how it handles transactions, and why it is a staple in the mainframe world.

Chapter 8: Transaction Management in DB2 Here, we delve into the specifics of transaction management in DB2, one of the most widely used database systems on mainframes. We will discuss how DB2 ensures the ACID properties of transactions, the techniques it uses for concurrency control, and how it handles recovery.

Chapter 9: IMS Transaction Management In this chapter, we explore transaction management in the Information Management System (IMS), another critical mainframe database system. We will understand how IMS transactions work, how IMS ensures data integrity and consistency, and its approach to concurrency control and recovery.

Chapter 10: Middleware in Mainframe Transaction Processing The final chapter of this part discusses the role of middleware in mainframe transaction processing. We will understand what middleware is, the different types of middleware used in mainframes, and how they facilitate communication and data exchange in a mainframe environment.

By the end of this part, readers will have a detailed understanding of the key components and processes involved in mainframe transaction processing, preparing them to work effectively with these powerful systems.

Chapter 7: Understanding CICS - Customer Information Control System

—

7.1 Introduction to CICS This section introduces the reader to CICS, including a brief history, its role in the mainframe ecosystem, and why it is important in the context of transaction processing.

7.2 Architecture of CICS A deeper dive into the architectural components of CICS, explaining its structure, key components, and how it facilitates transaction processing on mainframes.

7.3 Key Concepts in CICS This section elucidates the key concepts in CICS, including programs, transactions, resources, and the different types of processing, such as pseudo-conversational processing.

7.4 Transaction Processing in CICS A detailed discussion on how CICS handles transaction processing. Topics include the CICS command level interface, the process of defining and installing resources, and the transaction scheduling and dispatching process.

7.5 CICS and Databases A discussion on how CICS interacts with databases in the mainframe ecosystem. This section discusses the various database management systems CICS can work with, and how it facilitates database transactions.

7.6 CICS and Programming Languages This part discusses the interaction of various programming languages with CICS, covering languages like COBOL, Java, and C/C++, and how they can be used to develop CICS applications.

7.7 CICS Tools and Utilities A walkthrough of some of the common tools and utilities that developers and administrators use when working with CICS.

7.8 CICS in the Modern Era This section discusses the role of CICS in modern mainframe usage, covering topics like web services, CICS bundles, and the new challenges and opportunities presented by cloud computing and distributed systems.

7.9 Conclusion The chapter wraps up with a summary of the key points covered and a reflection on the significance of CICS in mainframe transaction processing.

7.1 Introduction to CICS

IN THE WORLD OF MAINFRAME transaction processing, few components are as vital as the Customer Information Control System (CICS). CICS is a transaction server that enables the development, execution, and management of applications for online transaction processing (OLTP).

Created by IBM in the 1960s, CICS has evolved and innovated alongside the IT industry, adapting to new technologies and paradigms while remaining a trusted and reliable tool for mission-critical applications worldwide. Its rich history includes a continuous track of performance enhancements, functionality expansions, and compatibility inclusions for new programming languages, keeping it relevant in the modern computing landscape.

CICS plays a central role in the mainframe ecosystem, serving as the interface between users and mainframe resources. It manages the execution of applications, ensuring they perform efficiently and securely, and that they maintain data consistency even in high-volume, concurrent transaction environments.

The importance of CICS is underscored by its ubiquitous presence in industries that depend heavily on reliable and scalable transaction processing. From banking and finance to retail and healthcare, many of the world's largest enterprises trust CICS for their most critical applications. It is instrumental in processing billions of transactions daily, demonstrating its resilience, performance, and value to businesses around the globe.

Understanding CICS, therefore, is a key aspect of mastering mainframe transaction processing. Its robust architecture, diverse features, and deep integration with mainframe databases and programming languages make it an indispensable tool for anyone working with mainframes.

7.2 Architecture of CICS

THE ARCHITECTURE OF the Customer Information Control System (CICS) is key to understanding how it handles transaction processing on mainframes.

CICS operates in a region – a protected area of memory – within the mainframe's operating system. Each region can run multiple transactions concurrently, efficiently using the mainframe's resources. The architecture of CICS can be understood in terms of its main components:

1. Transaction Manager: This component coordinates the execution of transactions. It ensures that transactions run to completion and are either committed if successful or rolled back if an error occurs, maintaining the ACID properties of transactions (Atomicity, Consistency, Isolation, Durability).

2. Resource Managers: These components manage the various resources used by transactions. This includes databases, message queues, and devices like terminals. They also handle the locking and unlocking of resources to maintain data consistency.

3. Application Programs: These are the actual business applications that run within CICS. They can be written in various languages, including COBOL, Java, and C/C++. These programs use CICS commands to access and manipulate resources.

4. Security Manager: The Security Manager controls access to resources based on predefined security policies. It plays a crucial role in ensuring that only authorized users and programs can access and modify data.

5. Storage Manager: This component manages the memory of the CICS region, ensuring efficient use of available memory and preventing memory leaks which could impact performance.

6. Task Manager: The Task Manager manages the multiple concurrent tasks (i.e., transactions) that can be running in a CICS region. It handles task scheduling and dispatching, and maintains isolation between tasks.

These components work together to process transactions in a highly efficient, secure, and reliable manner. By effectively managing resources and coordinating transaction execution, CICS enables mainframes to process large volumes of transactions with high performance and reliability.

7.3 Key Concepts in CICS

THIS SECTION DELVES into some of the key concepts integral to understanding CICS and its operation.

1. Programs: In CICS, a program is a self-contained unit of logic, usually written in a language like COBOL or Java. It can perform a specific task or a set of related tasks. Programs can be invoked by transactions and can use CICS commands to perform operations such as reading from or writing to a database.

2. Transactions: A transaction in CICS is a unit of work, initiated by a user or an application, that accomplishes a particular business function. For example, a banking transaction may involve withdrawing money from an account. Each transaction is associated with a unique transaction identifier (TranID), which is a four-character code.

3. Resources: Resources in CICS can be anything that a program interacts with, such as data files, databases, or devices like terminals. Resource managers within CICS are responsible for controlling access to these resources, ensuring data consistency and integrity.

4. Pseudo-conversational processing: Pseudo-conversational processing is a programming technique used in CICS to manage system resources efficiently. Instead of keeping a conversation with a user open (and tying up system resources) for the whole duration of a multi-step transaction, CICS ends the conversation after each step, freeing up resources. When the user is ready for the next step, the conversation is resumed, and the process continues. This allows CICS to handle large numbers of

users concurrently, without overloading system resources.

Understanding these key concepts provides a solid foundation for delving deeper into the functionality and capabilities of CICS.

7.4 Transaction Processing in CICS

THIS SECTION PROVIDES a detailed exploration of how transaction processing is handled in CICS.

1. CICS Command Level Interface: CICS uses a command level interface, which allows programs to interact with resources like databases or devices through a set of predefined commands. These commands cover a range of operations, such as sending or receiving data from a device, starting or ending a unit of work, or handling errors. The command level interface abstracts the underlying complexities, allowing programmers to focus on the business logic.

2. Defining and Installing Resources: Before a resource (like a file or a database) can be used by a CICS program, it needs to be defined to CICS using Resource Definition Online (RDO) or the older method, CICS table definitions. Once defined, the resource is installed into CICS, which makes it available for use. The process of defining and installing resources helps manage access to these resources, providing control over who can use them and how they can be used.

3. Transaction Scheduling and Dispatching: When a request to start a transaction is received, CICS first checks if the transaction is defined and enabled. If it is, the transaction is put into a queue for processing. The CICS scheduler then dispatches the transaction to an available task control block (TCB), which is a data structure that represents a unit of work in the system. The TCB runs the program associated with the transaction, executing its logic until the transaction is complete or an error occurs.

Understanding the intricacies of transaction processing in CICS is vital, as it forms the backbone of many mainframe applications, enabling high volume, reliable, and efficient transaction processing.

7.5 CICS and Databases

CICS PLAYS A SIGNIFICANT role in interacting with databases for transaction processing in the mainframe ecosystem. CICS has the capability to work with various database management systems (DBMS), and its integration with databases is essential for performing various tasks and operations.

1. DB2: DB2 is a relational DBMS from IBM and is widely used with CICS. CICS provides efficient, concurrent, and secure access to DB2 databases, taking care of connection management, transaction synchronization, and error recovery. A CICS program can access DB2 using SQL embedded in COBOL or PL/I programs.

2. IMS DB: IMS DB is a hierarchical DBMS also from IBM. Like with DB2, CICS programs can access IMS databases, with CICS ensuring synchronization between IMS transactions and CICS transactions, and managing access to IMS resources.

3. VSAM: VSAM (Virtual Storage Access Method) is a file storage access method used on IBM mainframes. CICS can use VSAM datasets as databases, managing the record-level locking and allowing multiple programs to access the data concurrently.

CICS also supports other databases, such as Oracle and SQL Server, on a mainframe or a distributed system.

CICS manages database transactions following the ACID properties (Atomicity, Consistency, Isolation, Durability) to ensure data integrity and reliability. It coordinates with the DBMS to start and end database transactions, manages commit and rollback operations, and handles any errors or exceptions that occur during the transaction processing.

Understanding the relationship between CICS and databases provides a more comprehensive picture of how transaction processing happens on mainframes, given that databases are often the primary resource accessed during a transaction.

7.6 CICS and Programming Languages

CICS INTERACTS WITH various programming languages to facilitate the development of transaction processing applications. Different languages are used depending on the needs of the application, the skillset of the development team, and the existing infrastructure.

1. COBOL: One of the most common languages used with CICS, COBOL (Common Business-Oriented Language) has been a mainstay of business computing for decades. It provides robust data handling capabilities and is particularly well-suited to processing large volumes of data. With CICS, developers can use COBOL to write programs that interact with users, manage transactions, and access databases.

2. Java: Java brings the benefits of object-oriented programming to the mainframe environment. CICS fully supports Java, allowing developers to write CICS applications in Java, use Java libraries and frameworks, and leverage the Java ecosystem. With the JCICS (Java Classes for CICS) API, Java programs can interact with CICS resources, manage transactions, and communicate with other programs.

3. C/C++: CICS also supports C and C++, allowing developers to write high-performance applications and take advantage of the powerful features these languages offer. The CICS C/C++ API provides functions for interacting with CICS resources, managing transactions, and more.

In addition to these languages, CICS also supports others like PL/I and Assembler. No matter what language is used, developers can leverage CICS's powerful transaction management capabilities to build robust, scalable, and efficient mainframe applications.

7.7 CICS Tools and Utilities

CICS PROVIDES A RANGE of tools and utilities to aid developers and administrators in the management of transactions and application development. Here's a look at some of the key tools:

1. CICS Explorer: CICS Explorer is a powerful, GUI-based tool that provides a comprehensive view of CICS regions. It simplifies resource definition, deployment, and management tasks. Administrators can use it to browse and modify CICS resources, while developers can use it for debugging and application deployment.

2. CICS Transaction Gateway (CICS TG): CICS TG provides secure and reliable connectivity between CICS systems and a range of applications, from modern web-based applications to traditional enterprise applications. It supports multiple communication protocols, including TCP/IP, HTTP, and Web Services, facilitating integration with diverse systems.

3. CICS Interdependency Analyzer: This tool helps administrators understand the relationships between different CICS resources. It is useful for assessing the impact of changes and managing the complexity of large CICS environments.

4. CICS Performance Analyzer: This tool provides detailed analysis of CICS system and application performance. It helps identify performance bottlenecks and optimize system performance.

5. CICS Debugging Tools: Debugging tools like CEDF (CICS Execution Diagnostic Facility) and CEDX (CICS Execution Diagnostic Exit) allow developers to examine program execution, assisting in troubleshooting and

problem-solving.

6. CICS Configuration Manager: It is a tool that provides version control and auditing for CICS resource definitions, helping to manage changes in complex CICS environments.

These tools, alongside others provided by CICS and third-party vendors, form an ecosystem that supports the development, deployment, and maintenance of CICS applications.

CICS provides a range of tools and utilities to aid developers and administrators in the management of transactions and application development. Here's a look at some of the key tools:

1. CICS Explorer: CICS Explorer is a powerful, GUI-based tool that provides a comprehensive view of CICS regions. It simplifies resource definition, deployment, and management tasks. Administrators can use it to browse and modify CICS resources, while developers can use it for debugging and application deployment.

2. CICS Transaction Gateway (CICS TG): CICS TG provides secure and reliable connectivity between CICS systems and a range of applications, from modern web-based applications to traditional enterprise applications. It supports multiple communication protocols, including TCP/IP, HTTP, and Web Services, facilitating integration with diverse systems.

3. CICS Interdependency Analyzer: This tool helps administrators understand the relationships between different CICS resources. It is useful for assessing the impact of changes and managing the complexity of large CICS environments.

4. CICS Performance Analyzer: This tool provides detailed

analysis of CICS system and application performance. It helps identify performance bottlenecks and optimize system performance.

5. CICS Debugging Tools: Debugging tools like CEDF (CICS Execution Diagnostic Facility) and CEDX (CICS Execution Diagnostic Exit) allow developers to examine program execution, assisting in troubleshooting and problem-solving.

6. CICS Configuration Manager: It is a tool that provides version control and auditing for CICS resource definitions, helping to manage changes in complex CICS environments.

These tools, alongside others provided by CICS and third-party vendors, form an ecosystem that supports the development, deployment, and maintenance of CICS applications.

7.8 CICS in the Modern Era

"CICS IN THE MODERN Era" covers the evolution of CICS to meet the challenges and opportunities of the present-day IT landscape.

1. Web Services and CICS: With the rise of the Internet and digital services, CICS has adapted to support web services, which allow CICS applications to communicate over the internet using standard protocols such as HTTP and SOAP. This feature enables CICS applications to seamlessly integrate with other applications, regardless of their platform or language, expanding the reach and interoperability of mainframe applications.

2. CICS Bundles: In the era of modular development and microservices, CICS bundles offer a way to package and deploy a group of related resources as a single unit. This promotes modular application design and facilitates application lifecycle management.

3. CICS and Cloud Computing: Cloud computing's scalability, elasticity, and service-oriented model present both challenges and opportunities for CICS. CICS has been evolving to integrate with cloud environments, with features like the CICS Transaction Gateway providing a bridge between CICS and cloud applications. In addition, IBM now offers a CICS option in their IBM Cloud, allowing businesses to leverage the benefits of both mainframe and cloud computing.

4. CICS and Distributed Systems: As businesses are increasingly adopting distributed architectures, CICS has also evolved to operate in these environments. It offers support for distributed transactions, helping ensure

consistency across distributed databases. Furthermore, CICS can serve as a key part of a distributed application, processing transactions from a variety of sources.

5. CICS and Containerization: As the world moves towards containerized deployments for software applications, CICS has kept pace by introducing CICS Containers and support for Docker, making it possible to containerize CICS applications for increased deployment flexibility and efficiency.

In the modern era, CICS continues to be a critical piece of the mainframe puzzle, evolving and adapting to meet the needs of today's businesses. By integrating with new technologies and trends, it ensures that mainframes remain relevant and continue to offer compelling solutions for high-volume transaction processing.

7.9 Conclusion

THE "CONCLUSION" OF chapter 7 draws together the main points discussed throughout the chapter, and underscores the importance of CICS in the mainframe landscape.

1. Understanding CICS: The chapter starts by introducing CICS, a middleware designed to support rapid, high-volume online transaction processing. It has evolved over the years to become a crucial element in the mainframe world.

2. CICS Architecture: A deeper exploration into the structure of CICS helps us understand how its design and components enable efficient transaction management.

3. Key Concepts: The discussion of concepts such as programs, transactions, and resources provides the necessary foundation to grasp how CICS functions.

4. Transaction Processing: The chapter then explores how CICS manages transaction processing, emphasizing the processes of defining, installing, scheduling, and dispatching resources.

5. CICS and Databases: An important aspect is how CICS interacts with different database management systems, facilitating database transactions in the mainframe environment.

6. CICS and Programming Languages: CICS's interaction with different programming languages like COBOL, Java, and C/C++ is vital to the development of CICS applications.

7. CICS Tools and Utilities: The walkthrough of various tools and utilities provides insight into the resources available for developers and administrators working with

CICS.
8. CICS in the Modern Era: The final section looks at how CICS has evolved to meet contemporary IT demands, including web services, cloud computing, and distributed systems.

The conclusion highlights that the versatility, resilience, and robust transaction processing capabilities of CICS make it a valuable asset in mainframes, reiterating its significant role in transaction processing and mainframe usage today.

Chapter 8: Transaction Management in DB2

———

8.1 Introduction to DB2 Transaction Management: This section provides an overview of transaction management in DB2, explaining its role in maintaining data integrity and consistency in a mainframe environment.

8.2 Understanding DB2 Transactions: Here we delve deeper into what constitutes a DB2 transaction, and the characteristics that make them ACID-compliant.

8.3 DB2 Locking Mechanisms: This part covers how DB2 manages concurrent transactions using locking mechanisms to prevent conflicts and ensure data consistency.

8.4 Isolation Levels in DB2: Different isolation levels in DB2 allow fine-tuning of the balance between data consistency and transaction performance. This section explains the various isolation levels and when to use them.

8.5 Logging and Recovery in DB2: One of the essential aspects of transaction management is the ability to recover data in case of failures. This part discusses how DB2 uses logging mechanisms for transaction recovery.

8.6 Distributed Transactions in DB2: This section covers the management of distributed transactions, which span across multiple databases or systems, in DB2.

8.7 Performance Tuning in DB2 Transaction Management: This part of the chapter focuses on strategies for performance tuning and optimization of DB2 transactions.

8.8 DB2 Transaction Management in the Modern Mainframe World: The chapter concludes with a look at how DB2 transaction management fits into modern mainframe usage and the ongoing evolution of mainframe technology.

8.9 Conclusion: This section provides a summary of the key points discussed in the chapter and reflects on the significance of transaction management in DB2 for maintaining data integrity and consistency in a mainframe environment.

8.1 Introduction to DB2 Transaction Management

IN THE INTRODUCTORY section of DB2 Transaction Management, we discuss the fundamentals of transaction management in IBM's DB2 database system, particularly in the context of a mainframe environment.

In any database system, a transaction is a sequence of one or more operations (such as read, update, insert, or delete) that is executed as a single, indivisible unit of work. DB2, being a relational database system, follows the ACID properties (Atomicity, Consistency, Isolation, and Durability) for transaction management, which are crucial for maintaining data integrity and consistency.

Atomicity: This property ensures that a transaction is treated as a single, indivisible unit. This means that either all operations within the transaction are completed successfully, or none of them are. If any operation within the transaction fails, the entire transaction is rolled back, and the database remains unchanged.

Consistency: This property ensures that a transaction brings the database from one valid state to another. The database starts in a consistent state, and after the transaction is completed, it ends up in a consistent state again, even if intermediate states during the transaction are inconsistent.

Isolation: This property ensures that concurrent transactions do not interfere with each other. Each transaction is executed in isolation from others, meaning that the operations of one transaction are not visible to others until the transaction is committed.

Durability: This property ensures that once a transaction is committed, its changes are permanent and survive any subsequent system failures.

In the mainframe environment, where the volume of transactions is immense and the necessity for accuracy is paramount, these properties are of utmost importance. DB2 transaction management provides the necessary mechanisms and tools to ensure that these properties are adhered to. This not only ensures the integrity and consistency of data but also increases the reliability and efficiency of the mainframe systems.

8.2 Understanding DB2 Transactions

IN THE CONTEXT OF DB2, a transaction, also known as a unit of work (UOW), represents a sequence of SQL operations that are executed as a single unit. This can include operations such as inserting new data, updating or deleting existing data, or querying data from the database. Here are some of the fundamental concepts of DB2 transactions:

Begin Transaction: A transaction in DB2 begins with the first executable SQL statement. DB2 automatically starts a transaction for each SQL statement that can change data, such as INSERT, UPDATE, DELETE, or SELECT with FOR UPDATE.

End Transaction: A DB2 transaction ends when it is explicitly committed or rolled back by the application, or when an unhandled error or exception occurs.

DB2 transactions are designed to be ACID-compliant, meaning they adhere to the principles of Atomicity, Consistency, Isolation, and Durability:

Atomicity: DB2 ensures atomicity by treating each transaction as a single unit of work. If a transaction is interrupted (for example, due to a system failure or because of an error in one of the SQL statements), DB2 automatically rolls back any changes made during the transaction, ensuring that the database remains in a consistent state.

Consistency: DB2 maintains consistency by enforcing integrity constraints on the data. These constraints can be defined by the database schema (for example, primary and foreign key constraints) or by the application (through check constraints or triggers). If a transaction would violate any of these constraints, DB2 rejects the transaction, ensuring the database remains consistent.

Isolation: DB2 uses various mechanisms, such as locks and timestamps, to provide isolation between concurrent transactions. This means that each transaction operates on a consistent snapshot of the database, and the intermediate results of a transaction are not visible to other transactions until the transaction is committed.

Durability: Once a transaction is committed, DB2 ensures that the changes made by the transaction are permanent and will survive any subsequent system failures. This is achieved by writing the transaction's changes to a transaction log, which can be used to recover the committed transactions in case of a system failure.

Understanding these concepts is crucial for managing and optimizing transaction processing in a DB2 environment.

8.3 DB2 Locking Mechanisms

THE FUNDAMENTAL PRINCIPLE behind transaction processing is to ensure that multiple users can access and update shared data concurrently without conflicts, and the database maintains its consistency. DB2 accomplishes this with its locking mechanisms, which balance the need for concurrent access with the need to prevent conflicts.

Locks: At its core, a lock is a mechanism that prevents certain types of access to a resource by one transaction while that resource is being accessed by another transaction. DB2 automatically acquires and releases locks as necessary when a transaction is running. Locks can be applied at different levels of granularity, such as table, page, or row, with each level providing a different balance of concurrency and lock overhead.

Lock Modes: DB2 has several lock modes, including shared (S), update (U), and exclusive (X). Shared locks allow multiple transactions to read (but not change) the same resource. Update locks are a special type of lock used when a transaction intends to modify a resource and are designed to prevent other transactions from also obtaining update locks on the same resource. Exclusive locks prevent any other transaction from accessing the resource.

Lock Escalation: To reduce the overhead of managing many locks, DB2 can escalate locks from a lower level of granularity to a higher one (for example, from row locks to table locks) when a transaction acquires more than a certain number of locks.

Deadlock and Timeout: Deadlocks occur when two or more transactions are waiting for each other to release locks, creating a cycle that cannot be broken. DB2 automatically detects and resolves deadlocks by rolling back one of the transactions, allowing the others to proceed. A timeout is another way of handling contention, where a transaction waiting for a lock is made to wait until the lock becomes available or until the waiting period, known as the timeout period, expires.

Isolation Levels: DB2 supports multiple transaction isolation levels that determine how locks are used. These isolation levels provide a trade-off between concurrency and data consistency. The isolation levels in DB2 are Repeatable Read, Read Stability, Cursor Stability, and Uncommitted Read.

Understanding DB2's locking mechanisms is essential for managing performance and avoiding conflicts during transaction processing.

8.4 Isolation Levels in DB2

ISOLATION LEVELS IN DB2 govern how transactions access data, and how locks are obtained and released during transaction processing. These levels provide a balance between data consistency, concurrency, and system performance. Here are the four isolation levels in DB2:

1. Repeatable Read (RR): The highest level of isolation, RR holds all locks acquired during a transaction until it completes, ensuring that if the same row is read multiple times within a transaction, it will always be the same. While this ensures the highest level of consistency, it can significantly impact performance and concurrency due to the extensive lock duration.

2. Read Stability (RS): This level also holds all read locks until the end of the transaction, ensuring that any data read during a transaction doesn't change for the duration of the transaction. However, unlike RR, it allows new rows to be added to the result set of previous queries, providing a balance between consistency and performance.

3. Cursor Stability (CS): A more relaxed level, CS only holds locks for the duration of the current row fetch, meaning that a row lock is released as soon as the application moves to the next row. This improves concurrency at the cost of consistency - a row could be updated by another transaction between subsequent reads within the same transaction.

4. Uncommitted Read (UR): The lowest level of isolation, UR doesn't acquire read locks, allowing data to be read that other transactions may not have committed. This means a transaction could read uncommitted data ('dirty read'), but

it provides the highest level of concurrency and
performance.

Choosing the right isolation level depends on the specific needs of
a transaction and the overall workload. RR or RS can be suitable
for transactions requiring high consistency, while CS or UR can be
used in applications where performance and concurrency are more
critical. Remember that a higher isolation level typically means less
concurrency and potentially more locking contention, so always
choose the least restrictive isolation that still meets your consistency
needs.

8.5 Logging and Recovery in DB2

DB2 USES A SYSTEM OF logging to ensure that data can be recovered in the event of a system failure. This mechanism plays a critical role in the durability aspect of the ACID properties, enabling transactions to be rolled back or rolled forward to maintain data integrity and consistency. Here's how DB2 manages logging and recovery:

1. Logging: When a transaction is executed, DB2 records all changes made to the database in a transaction log. This log includes before and after images of the data, along with other details like the transaction ID and timestamp. There are two types of logs - the active log, which stores information about active or recently committed transactions, and the archive log, which stores older transactions and is used for long-term storage and recovery.

2. Write-Ahead Logging: DB2 uses a write-ahead logging (WAL) protocol. This means that before any changes to data are written to the database (on disk), the corresponding log record must be saved in the log (also on disk). This ensures that in the event of a failure, all actions of a transaction can be replayed from the log to bring the database to a consistent state.

3. Recovery: If a system failure occurs, DB2 uses the transaction logs to restore the database to a consistent state. It uses a two-step process - rollforward and rollback. The rollforward step replays the logs from the last backup to the point of failure, applying all changes to get to the most recent state. The rollback step then undoes any uncommitted transactions that were present at the point of failure, ensuring only committed transactions persist.

4. Checkpointing: DB2 uses a technique called checkpointing to minimize the time taken for recovery. At regular intervals (checkpoints), the database writes a special record to the log, detailing the state of all active transactions. In the event of recovery, DB2 can start from the most recent checkpoint rather than the beginning of the log, significantly speeding up the recovery process.

5. Log Sequence Number (LSN): Each log record is assigned a unique LSN, which represents a specific point in time in the database's history. LSNs are used during recovery to identify and sequence log records.

By using these mechanisms, DB2 can recover data efficiently and effectively, ensuring the durability of transactions and the integrity and consistency of the data.

8.6 Distributed Transactions in DB2

DISTRIBUTED TRANSACTIONS in DB2 refer to those transactions that span across multiple databases or systems. These types of transactions are essential in a networked or distributed computing environment, where data may be spread across various locations. Managing such transactions can be complex due to the increased coordination required to maintain data integrity and consistency across different databases.

Here's how DB2 handles distributed transactions:

1. Two-Phase Commit Protocol: DB2 utilizes the two-phase commit protocol to ensure atomicity and consistency across all participating databases in a distributed transaction. The protocol has two stages:
   - Prepare Phase: In this phase, each participating database is asked to promise to commit or abort the transaction, even if there is a system failure. If a database cannot make this promise (for example, due to a constraint violation), it can abort the transaction. The database makes necessary modifications and locks resources, but it does not yet make the changes permanent.
   - Commit Phase: If all databases have promised to commit, the transaction coordinator sends a 'commit' message to all of them. Each database makes the transaction's changes permanent and releases all locks. If any database has decided to abort the transaction in the prepare phase, a 'rollback' message is sent to all databases, and the transaction's changes are undone.

2. Distributed Unit of Work (UOW): In DB2, a distributed transaction is often referred to as a distributed unit of work. The application or transaction manager starts a unit of work, makes updates to one or more databases, and then either commits the unit of work (making all changes permanent across all databases) or rolls back the unit of work (undoing all changes).

3. Distributed Relational Database Architecture (DRDA): DB2 uses DRDA, a set of protocols for distributed data access across heterogeneous systems, to facilitate distributed transactions. DRDA supports communication and data exchange between DB2 and other DRDA-compliant databases.

4. Recovery and Consistency: In case of a failure during a distributed transaction, DB2 uses the two-phase commit protocol and its logging mechanisms to ensure that all databases are brought back to a consistent state. DB2's recovery facilities can handle the complexity of failures even in distributed environments.

By using these methods, DB2 effectively manages distributed transactions, ensuring that the ACID properties are maintained even when a transaction involves multiple databases or systems.

8.7 Performance Tuning in DB2 Transaction Management

PERFORMANCE TUNING in DB2 transaction management is critical for optimizing the system's resource utilization and enhancing the efficiency of database operations. This can have a significant impact on the system's overall performance and responsiveness, affecting how quickly and effectively transactions can be processed. Here are several strategies for performance tuning:

1. Optimal Locking Strategy: Implementing an optimal locking strategy can help to minimize lock contention, a situation in which multiple transactions are attempting to access the same data concurrently. Lock contention can lead to delays and reduce transaction throughput. Techniques such as lock size tuning (using smaller locks for tables with high concurrent access) and lock escalation thresholds can be utilized.

2. Isolation Level Tuning: Adjusting the isolation level in DB2 can balance the need for data consistency against the need for high performance. Lower isolation levels typically offer better performance but at the risk of reduced data consistency.

3. Buffer Pool Tuning: Buffer pools are areas of memory that hold database pages while they are being used. Performance can be improved by tuning the buffer pool hit ratio (the percentage of time that a page to be accessed is in the buffer pool), which reduces I/O operations.

4. Index and SQL Query Optimization: Optimizing the use of indexes can significantly speed up data retrieval in a transaction. Moreover, efficient SQL queries can reduce the load on the DB2 server, leading to faster transaction

processing. The DB2 Optimizer can assist in choosing the best access path for SQL statements.

5. Log Buffer Tuning: The log buffer is used to store log records before they're written to disk. A log buffer that's too small can limit the rate at which transactions can be committed, so adjusting the size of this buffer can help improve performance.

6. Using Stored Procedures: Stored procedures allow for the execution of SQL statements in the DB2 server itself, reducing the overhead of communication between an application and DB2.

7. Distributed Data Management: For distributed transactions, network latency can be a significant factor affecting performance. Techniques such as query parallelism and multi-system transactions can be used to improve distributed transaction performance.

Remember, every DB2 environment is unique, and what works in one situation might not work in another. Regular monitoring and performance testing should be a part of the DB2 system's lifecycle, allowing for continuous performance optimization.

8.8 DB2 Transaction Management in the Modern Mainframe World

DB2 TRANSACTION MANAGEMENT remains an essential component in the modern mainframe world. As businesses handle more complex and data-intensive tasks, the features and functions provided by DB2 to ensure data integrity and transaction reliability are more important than ever. Here are some of the ways DB2 transaction management fits into the current landscape:

1. Integration with Modern Technologies: DB2 has evolved alongside other technologies. For instance, it now integrates with languages such as Java, Python, and JavaScript, allowing for the development of complex, high-performing applications that can leverage the robust transaction management capabilities of DB2. It can also work with web-based technologies for internet-based applications and services.

2. In the Era of Big Data: With the explosion of data in recent years, businesses require databases that can handle a high volume of transactions and large datasets. DB2's advanced transaction management capabilities make it an excellent choice for big data applications. It can handle large volumes of data and high transaction rates, ensuring that data remains consistent and recoverable, essential in big data applications.

3. Cloud and Hybrid Environments: DB2 is not limited to traditional on-premise mainframes but can also run in cloud and hybrid environments. This flexibility means that businesses can leverage DB2's transaction management capabilities in various setups, from traditional mainframes to modern cloud-based systems.

4. AI and Machine Learning: Machine learning and AI are becoming integral parts of many businesses, and DB2 has features that support these advanced technologies. For example, IBM has integrated Db2 with IBM Watson technology for AI-driven database management.

5. Security: As cybersecurity threats grow, so does the need for secure transaction processing. DB2 provides robust security features, such as encryption and access control mechanisms, to ensure that transactions are secure.

The ongoing evolution of DB2 and mainframe technology ensures that DB2 transaction management will remain a crucial component in the data strategies of many businesses in the future. As DB2 continues to evolve and integrate with new technologies, it will continue to provide a reliable, robust, and high-performing platform for transaction management.

8.9 Conclusion

THIS CHAPTER PRESENTED an in-depth view of transaction management in DB2, demonstrating its importance in maintaining data integrity and consistency in a mainframe environment. DB2's robust transaction management capabilities provide the framework needed to support secure, reliable, and efficient transactions, a fundamental requirement in today's data-intensive business operations.

Key points covered in this chapter include:

1. DB2 Transactions: We explored the concept of DB2 transactions, highlighting their ACID properties—atomicity, consistency, isolation, and durability—which are central to ensuring data integrity in transaction processing.

2. DB2 Locking Mechanisms: We discussed DB2's use of locking mechanisms, which manage concurrent transactions and prevent conflicts, ultimately safeguarding data consistency.

3. Isolation Levels in DB2: The various isolation levels in DB2 allow for the adjustment of the balance between data consistency and transaction performance. Choosing the right isolation level is critical in optimizing the performance of your DB2 applications.

4. Logging and Recovery: We delved into how DB2 uses logging mechanisms for transaction recovery—an essential process that safeguards data in the event of failures.

5. Distributed Transactions: The chapter explored how DB2 handles transactions that span across multiple databases or systems.

6. Performance Tuning: The strategies for performance tuning and optimization of DB2 transactions, a crucial aspect for enhancing the efficiency of data processing in an organization, were discussed.

7. Modern Mainframe World: Lastly, we examined how DB2 fits into the modern mainframe landscape, emphasizing how its robust transaction management capabilities remain crucial in the face of evolving technologies and increasing data volumes.

DB2's powerful transaction management is one of the reasons why it remains a leading choice for organizations operating in mainframe environments. As technologies and business needs continue to evolve, DB2 continues to provide the robustness and reliability required for handling business-critical data and transactions. This underlines the significance of understanding and effectively leveraging DB2 transaction management in any data strategy involving mainframes.

Chapter 9: IMS Transaction Management

9.1 Introduction to IMS Transaction Management A brief overview of IMS transaction management and its significance in mainframe environments.

9.2 The Structure of IMS Transactions A look at the architecture of IMS transactions, including the components involved and how they interact.

9.3 Transaction Processing in IMS An in-depth exploration of how IMS processes transactions, discussing concepts such as message queuing, scheduling, and synchronization.

9.4 IMS and Databases This section discusses how IMS interfaces with databases, with particular focus on its hierarchical database model.

9.5 IMS Transaction Isolation and Recovery Here we delve into how IMS achieves transaction isolation and how it recovers from failures to ensure data integrity and consistency.

9.6 IMS and Programming Languages An examination of how various programming languages, such as COBOL and Java, can be used to develop IMS applications.

9.7 IMS Tools and Utilities A walkthrough of some of the tools and utilities used when working with IMS.

9.8 IMS in the Modern Mainframe World This section takes a look at the role of IMS in contemporary mainframe usage, discussing how it has evolved to meet the demands of modern applications.

9.9 Conclusion The chapter wraps up with a summary of the key points discussed and a reflection on the importance of understanding IMS transaction management in a mainframe environment.

9.1 Introduction to IMS Transaction Management

THE IBM INFORMATION Management System (IMS) is a crucial component in the mainframe environment due to its high-efficiency transaction processing and hierarchical database management capabilities. A mainframe application typically comprises thousands to millions of transactions that need to be processed swiftly and efficiently, often in real-time, which is where IMS comes into play.

IMS transaction management (IMS TM) is a component of the IMS system responsible for processing transactions from a variety of sources, including online users, applications, and other programs. It offers powerful facilities to manage these transactions effectively, ensuring speed, consistency, and recovery capabilities, crucial elements in maintaining the integrity of business operations.

IMS TM works on a messaging model where transactions are processed as messages. These messages are stored in queues until they can be processed. This model allows for excellent scalability and robustness, as the system can continue to accept messages even if the processing slows down, providing high availability.

As businesses increasingly rely on real-time data and fast response times, IMS's ability to handle large volumes of transactions quickly and accurately makes it an essential part of mainframe environments. Understanding how IMS transaction management works is crucial for designing, implementing, and maintaining efficient mainframe systems that meet the demanding requirements of modern businesses. This chapter will delve deeper into the intricacies of IMS transaction management and its vital role in the mainframe ecosystem.

9.2 The Structure of IMS Transactions

IMS TRANSACTIONS ARE central to IMS's high-speed, high-volume processing capabilities. A transaction in the context of IMS involves a single logical unit of work, such as updating a customer's address or processing a purchase order.

An IMS transaction consists of several fundamental components that work together to facilitate transaction processing. These components include:

1. Message Queues: IMS uses a message-driven processing model. Transactions in IMS are processed as messages that are placed in a message queue. When a user or application initiates a transaction, IMS packages the input into a message and puts it in a queue for processing.

2. Message Processing Programs (MPPs): These are the application programs that process the transactions. When a message reaches the front of its queue, IMS wakes up an MPP to process the transaction. After processing, the MPP can send a reply message back to the user or application.

3. Transaction Scheduler: The transaction scheduler is the part of IMS that manages the execution of transactions. It controls which transactions are currently being processed, assigns transactions to MPPs, and manages the allocation of system resources.

4. IMS Control Program: This is the main part of IMS that oversees the entire transaction processing flow. It manages the message queues, coordinates with the transaction scheduler, and communicates with the MPPs to process transactions.

5. Data Language Interface (DL/I): DL/I is the

programming interface that MPPs use to interact with the
IMS database. It provides a set of calls that programs can
use to manipulate data in an IMS database as part of a
transaction.

Each component plays a critical role in the overall transaction flow.
Understanding the structure and interactions of these components is
vital to understanding how IMS manages to process high volumes of
transactions quickly and accurately.

9.3 Transaction Processing in IMS

IMS TRANSACTION PROCESSING is a combination of several steps that are meticulously coordinated to ensure high performance and reliability. The main concepts involved in this process include message queuing, scheduling, and synchronization. Let's discuss these concepts further:

1. Message Queuing: In IMS, all transactions are initiated as messages, and these messages are placed in a message queue. A message could be anything from a simple request for data to a complex update involving multiple records. This method allows for both batch processing and real-time transaction processing. When a message enters the system, IMS places it in the appropriate queue based on the transaction's priority level.

2. Scheduling: The scheduling process in IMS is an essential part of its transaction processing mechanism. The IMS Transaction Manager (TM) is responsible for scheduling the transactions. The TM assigns a Message Processing Program (MPP) to each transaction in the queue based on the transaction code embedded in the message. It ensures that sufficient system resources are available for each MPP to execute its task. The TM also handles task-switching efficiently to allow for high-volume transaction processing.

3. Synchronization: Ensuring that all parts of a transaction are completed successfully is crucial to maintaining data integrity. If one part of the transaction fails, the entire transaction must be rolled back to maintain consistency. IMS manages this through a process known as synchronization. It uses a technique called "backout" which can undo operations that are part of an incomplete

transaction, thus ensuring the Atomicity (the "A" in ACID properties) of transactions.

4. Recovery and Restart: To ensure the durability of transactions (the "D" in ACID), IMS has sophisticated recovery and restart procedures. If a system failure occurs during transaction processing, IMS can restart the system from a known consistent point and recover the in-flight transactions to ensure data integrity.

5. Concurrency Control: To handle concurrent transactions, IMS uses different locking strategies. It allows concurrent read operations but uses locks to prevent multiple transactions from updating the same data simultaneously.

In a nutshell, the transaction processing in IMS is designed to manage high-volume, high-speed transaction workloads efficiently. By using techniques such as message queuing, scheduling, synchronization, recovery, and concurrency control, IMS can deliver the fast, reliable transaction processing that businesses need.

9.4 IMS and Databases

IBM'S INFORMATION MANAGEMENT System (IMS) is an integrated database and transaction management system that was designed to work with its own database model, the hierarchical database model. This model and its interaction with IMS form an essential aspect of mainframe transaction processing.

The hierarchical database model is a structure of data that is organized into a tree-like format, where one parent node can have multiple children, but each child has only one parent. The structure allows for efficient data processing and is well-suited for relationships where one entity can have many related entities but where the related entities are not related to each other.

1. IMS Database Manager: The IMS Database Manager (DB) is responsible for maintaining and providing access to IMS databases. When a transaction needs to read from or write to the database, the IMS DB facilitates this through a series of calls and commands, such as GET, PUT, and DELETE calls. The DB Manager is designed to handle the unique complexities of the hierarchical model, such as the need for parent-child navigation.

2. Hierarchical Databases in IMS: Hierarchical databases in IMS are organized into segments, with each segment representing a record. These segments are arranged into hierarchies, where a parent segment can have multiple child segments, but each child segment can only have one parent segment. This hierarchical structure is defined in the Database Description (DBD) for the database.

3. Data Access: To access data in the IMS hierarchical databases, applications use a series of DL/I (Data

Language/I) calls. These calls navigate the database hierarchy to retrieve, update, or delete data. The application's position within the hierarchy at any given time is known as its position of currency. IMS maintains this position of currency for each transaction, allowing it to pick up where it left off if the transaction is interrupted.

4. Synchronization and Locking: IMS uses synchronization techniques to ensure that transactions can be rolled back if necessary. IMS also uses a locking mechanism to ensure that when a transaction is updating data, other transactions can't access the same data, thereby preventing data inconsistencies.

The tight coupling of IMS and its hierarchical database model provides a robust and efficient way to manage complex transaction processing tasks. Despite being an older model, it still plays a vital role in many sectors, such as banking, where high-speed, high-volume transaction processing is required.

9.5 IMS Transaction Isolation and Recovery

IMS EMPLOYS A RANGE of strategies and techniques to achieve transaction isolation and recovery. The goals of these strategies are to ensure data integrity, maintain data consistency, and recover from failures when they occur.

1. Transaction Isolation: Transaction isolation is a critical aspect of any transaction management system. It ensures that the operations of one transaction are invisible to other concurrent transactions, thus preventing conflicts and maintaining data consistency. In IMS, isolation is achieved through the use of locking mechanisms. When a transaction is processing, IMS locks the segments of data it is accessing. These locks prevent other transactions from accessing the same data until the initial transaction is complete, thus achieving isolation.

2. Recovery: IMS uses logging and checkpointing to ensure that the system can recover from failures. Whenever a transaction makes changes to the database, IMS logs the changes in a log dataset. If the system fails before the transaction completes, the logged changes can be undone to restore the database to its previous state, a process known as backout recovery.

3. Checkpointing: In addition to logging, IMS uses checkpointing to minimize the amount of work needed for recovery. A checkpoint is a snapshot of the state of a transaction at a particular point in time. IMS periodically takes checkpoints during the processing of a transaction. If a failure occurs, recovery starts from the last checkpoint rather than from the beginning of the transaction, saving processing time.

4. Commit and Rollback: IMS also supports commit and rollback operations to ensure data integrity. If a transaction is processed successfully, it is committed, meaning all changes are finalized and written to the database. If a problem occurs during processing, the transaction is rolled back, and all changes made during the transaction are undone.

5. Restart and Recovery Manager (RRM): RRM in IMS controls the checkpointing, commit, and rollback operations. In case of any system or hardware failure, RRM initiates the recovery process from the last checkpoint.

By using these methods, IMS ensures that transactions are processed reliably and that data integrity and consistency are maintained even in the event of system failures.

9.6 IMS and Programming Languages

IMS TRANSACTION MANAGEMENT interfaces with several programming languages, allowing developers to create applications that interact with IMS databases. Two of the most commonly used languages in this context are COBOL and Java.

1. COBOL: One of the most extensively used programming languages in the mainframe environment, COBOL (Common Business-Oriented Language), is a high-level language that provides excellent file processing capabilities. In the context of IMS, COBOL is used to create programs that define the logic of the transactions. IMS provides a set of COBOL APIs that developers use to interact with IMS databases. These APIs allow programs to initiate transactions, read and update data in IMS databases, and handle errors.

2. Java: Java is another popular language for developing IMS applications. Java provides platform independence, which makes it a versatile choice for many organizations. IMS provides a comprehensive set of Java classes, interfaces, and methods that developers can use to interact with IMS databases and resources. With these tools, Java programs can initiate and manage IMS transactions, query and update IMS databases, and handle errors.

The choice of programming language can depend on various factors, such as the nature of the application, the skills of the development team, and the specific requirements of the project. Regardless of the language used, the goal is the same: to create robust applications that can effectively utilize the powerful transaction management capabilities of IMS.

9.7 IMS Tools and Utilities

THERE ARE A RANGE OF tools and utilities that developers and system administrators utilize when working with Information Management System (IMS) to create, manage, and optimize IMS applications and databases. Here are a few key ones:

1. IMS Database Solution Pack: This tool assists with the design, management, and maintenance of IMS databases. It includes features for database modeling, schema comparison, database administration, and performance analysis.

2. IMS Program Restart Facility: This utility helps manage and recover from system failures during application processing. If a system failure occurs, this tool enables IMS to restart the program at the point of interruption, avoiding the need to rerun the entire program.

3. IMS High Performance Unload and Load: These are utilities for quickly unloading data from an IMS database to a sequential data set, and loading data from a sequential data set into an IMS database, respectively. These tools are useful for backup and recovery processes, data migration, and reorganization tasks.

4. IMS Performance Analyzer: This tool provides comprehensive monitoring and analysis of IMS system performance. It helps in identifying bottlenecks, tuning the system for better performance, and planning capacity.

5. IBM Debug Tool for z/OS: This is a source-level debugging tool for IMS applications written in COBOL, PL/I, and other high-level languages. It helps developers to diagnose and fix application errors.

6. IBM Fault Analyzer for z/OS: When a program fails, this

tool collects diagnostic information to help identify the
cause of the failure. It can be used with IMS and other
mainframe subsystems.

Understanding and effectively using these tools can greatly enhance
the efficiency of working with IMS, facilitating improved
productivity and optimized performance of IMS applications and
databases.

9.8 IMS in the Modern Mainframe World

IMS (INFORMATION MANAGEMENT System) has long been a foundational technology in the mainframe world. Invented by IBM in the 1960s as part of the Apollo space program, IMS is a hierarchical database and transaction management system that is distinguished by its performance, reliability, and scalability.

With the advent of more modern data management systems, one might expect that IMS would have become obsolete. However, that's far from the case. IMS has been continuously evolved and updated by IBM to meet the demands of modern applications and business needs. Here's how IMS fits into the modern mainframe world:

1. Integration with Modern Technologies: IMS integrates with modern technologies such as Java and Web Services. You can build Java applications that run on IMS and utilize open-source technologies like JDBC (Java Database Connectivity) to interact with IMS databases. Additionally, IMS supports SOA (Service-Oriented Architecture), allowing IMS transactions to be wrapped as web services that can be accessed from anywhere in the world over the internet.

2. Support for Modern Development Practices: IMS supports modern development and operations practices, often known as DevOps. For example, there are tools that allow you to manage IMS code using Git, the popular version control system. IBM also offers a tool named Dependency Based Build, which provides a modern, script-based build environment for z/OS applications including IMS.

3. Enhanced Security: With the rising importance of data

security, IMS has incorporated robust security features to safeguard sensitive data. It supports Resource Access Control Facility (RACF) to secure access to resources, and provides SSL/TLS support for securing network communications. IBM has also added support for multi-factor authentication in IMS.

4. Performance Improvements: IBM has introduced various features to enhance IMS's performance and efficiency, such as High-Speed Sequential Processing (HSSP) for faster batch processing, and Shared Queues for improved workload balancing and system availability.

5. Modern Database Features: IMS now supports modern database features such as SQL access, making it easier for developers who are familiar with relational databases to work with IMS.

In conclusion, IMS continues to play a vital role in the modern mainframe world due to its robustness, scalability, and adaptability. While its core remains the same - providing efficient, reliable transaction and database management - its capabilities have expanded to support the requirements of modern applications. This ongoing evolution is a testament to the enduring value and versatility of IMS in a rapidly changing technology landscape.

9.9 Conclusion

IN THIS CHAPTER, WE have taken an in-depth look at IBM's Information Management System (IMS) and its role in mainframe transaction management. IMS is not just a relic from the early days of computing; it continues to be a critical component of many enterprise mainframe systems today. The reasons for this sustained relevance are manifold:

1. Hierarchical Database Model: IMS's hierarchical database model, though different from the commonly used relational model, offers advantages in terms of performance and efficiency for certain types of data and access patterns.

2. Transaction Processing: We delved into the intricacies of IMS's transaction processing mechanism, which is distinguished by its message queuing, scheduling, and synchronization capabilities. These aspects enable IMS to provide high performance and robustness in handling a large volume of transactions.

3. Interactions with Databases: Our exploration of how IMS interacts with databases demonstrated its versatility in managing and accessing data. Notably, IMS's integration with DB2 and its own hierarchical databases provides a high degree of flexibility in data management.

4. Recovery and Isolation: We discussed how IMS handles transaction isolation and recovery, key aspects of ensuring data integrity and consistency. IMS's robust mechanisms in these areas contribute to its reputation for reliability.

5. Programming Language Support: IMS's support for programming languages like COBOL and Java ensures that it can cater to a broad range of development requirements. This versatility enables developers to

leverage existing skills and tools to build and maintain IMS applications.

6. Modern Relevance: Finally, we highlighted how IMS continues to evolve to meet the demands of modern mainframe usage, including integration with modern technologies, enhanced security, and support for modern development practices.

In conclusion, understanding IMS transaction management is crucial for anyone working with mainframes, given its vital role in many mainframe environments. By combining historical robustness and performance with modern features and compatibility, IMS remains an essential pillar of mainframe transaction management.

Chapter 10: Middleware in Mainframe Transaction Processing

10<!---->.1 Introduction to Middleware: This section provides a brief introduction to the concept of middleware in the context of mainframe transaction processing, including its role and significance.

10.2 Types of Middleware: A look at the various types of middleware used in mainframe environments, including message-oriented middleware, application servers, and database access middleware.

10.3 Middleware in Transaction Processing: This part explores the role of middleware in transaction processing, discussing how it facilitates communication, data exchange, and coordination among various components.

10.4 Middleware and Databases: Here we discuss the interaction between middleware and databases, detailing how middleware assists in database connectivity, transaction management, and data translation.

10.5 Middleware and Mainframe Programming Languages: This section explains how middleware interacts with mainframe programming languages, providing interfaces for executing operations and handling transactions.

10.6 Middleware Tools and Utilities: A look at some of the tools and utilities that developers and administrators use in the context of middleware for mainframe transaction processing.

10.7 Middleware in the Modern Mainframe World: This part discusses how middleware is evolving to meet the demands of modern mainframe environments, including cloud computing, distributed systems, and service-oriented architectures.

10.8 Conclusion: The chapter wraps up with a summary of the key points discussed and a reflection on the role of middleware in mainframe transaction processing.

10.1 Introduction to Middleware

IN THE CONTEXT OF MAINFRAME transaction processing, middleware plays an integral role in enabling communication and interaction between different software components. Middleware can be considered as the "glue" that binds together disparate applications, allowing them to communicate and share data efficiently and reliably.

The main function of middleware is to provide abstraction and transparency, hiding the complexities of distributed processes from the user and the programmer. It helps to manage heterogeneity and the diversity of computer hardware, operating systems, network protocols, and programming languages that may exist within a mainframe environment.

In the realm of transaction processing, middleware provides important services such as transaction management, concurrency control, distribution transparency, and security, among others. These functions are crucial in coordinating and orchestrating the actions of individual components of a transactional system, ensuring that all parts work together seamlessly to process transactions efficiently and accurately.

Moreover, middleware helps to ensure the properties of ACID (Atomicity, Consistency, Isolation, Durability) in a transactional system. By managing transactions in such a way that they either completely succeed or fail as a whole (atomicity), maintaining a consistent state before and after the transaction (consistency), isolating the effects of a transaction from other transactions until it is complete (isolation), and guaranteeing that the effects of a completed transaction are permanent (durability), middleware plays a pivotal role in maintaining the integrity and reliability of mainframe transaction processing systems.

Understanding middleware is, therefore, crucial for any study of mainframe transaction processing as it provides the underlying support that enables efficient and reliable transaction processing. In the sections that follow, we will delve deeper into the different types of middleware, their roles in transaction processing, and how they interact with databases and mainframe programming languages.

10.2 Types of Middleware

THIS SECTION EXPLORES the different types of middleware commonly found in mainframe environments, offering an insight into their functions, capabilities, and their impact on transaction processing.

1. Message-Oriented Middleware (MOM): This type of middleware supports the exchange of general-purpose messages between different applications in a distributed system. MOM operates asynchronously, meaning that the sending and receiving applications do not need to interact with the message simultaneously. Key features include reliable delivery, routing, and transformation of messages. IBM MQ, formerly known as MQSeries, is a popular example of MOM in mainframe environments. In terms of transaction processing, MOM ensures that transactions are carried out smoothly and data integrity is maintained, even when communication is taking place between different applications and systems.

2. Application Servers: These are middleware platforms that provide a comprehensive service layer, including transaction management, security, clustering, and load balancing for building and deploying applications. They enable businesses to create, deploy, and manage business applications in a mainframe environment. Application servers like IBM's CICS and WebSphere are known for their ability to manage transactions efficiently, ensuring data integrity and system reliability.

3. Database Access Middleware: This type of middleware simplifies the process of interacting with databases by providing a consistent interface for different database

systems. It handles tasks such as connection pooling, transaction management, and query processing, hiding the complexity of these operations from the application. IBM's DB2 Connect is a typical example of database access middleware, allowing applications to interact with DB2 databases in a uniform way. In the context of transaction processing, database access middleware ensures that transactions involving databases are handled smoothly and efficiently, with minimal overhead.

Each type of middleware plays a unique role in a mainframe environment, and understanding their functions is key to grasping how transaction processing takes place in these powerful systems.

10.3 Middleware in Transaction Processing

IN THE CONTEXT OF MAINFRAME transaction processing, middleware serves as a crucial layer that sits between operating systems and applications. It provides common services and capabilities that allow disparate applications and services to communicate and exchange data efficiently and reliably, which is essential for smooth transaction processing.

1. Communication Facilitation: Middleware provides the communication infrastructure that allows applications and services to interact across a variety of network technologies and protocols. It abstracts the complexities of the underlying network, allowing developers to focus on business logic rather than communication details. This communication is critical in transaction processing, as it often involves multiple services and databases that need to interact.

2. Data Exchange: Middleware is responsible for translating data between different formats and ensuring that it's appropriately sent and received by various components. For instance, message-oriented middleware can convert messages into a standard format that can be read by different applications, ensuring that all parts of a transaction can understand the data being exchanged.

3. Transaction Coordination: Middleware plays a crucial role in coordinating and managing transactions that span multiple resources. It can handle tasks like managing distributed transactions, ensuring all parts of a transaction are completed or none at all (known as atomicity), and managing rollback and recovery in case of failure. This coordination is crucial in maintaining data integrity and

consistency, which are key in transaction processing.

4. Load Balancing and Scaling: Middleware can also handle load balancing and scaling, distributing transactions evenly across available resources to maximize efficiency and throughput. This capability is essential in high-volume transaction processing environments where performance and reliability are key.

5. Security: Middleware also plays a key role in securing transactions, providing features such as authentication, authorization, and encryption to protect sensitive data and ensure it's only accessible to authorized entities.

In essence, middleware is a key enabler of transaction processing in mainframe environments, providing the tools and infrastructure necessary to manage complex interactions and ensure that transactions are executed efficiently, reliably, and securely.

10.4 Middleware and Databases

MIDDLEWARE PLAYS A crucial role in enabling and managing the interaction between applications and databases in a mainframe environment, providing essential services and functionalities such as database connectivity, transaction management, and data translation.

1. Database Connectivity: Middleware provides an abstraction layer that simplifies the process of connecting to databases. This can include managing connection pooling (reusing database connections), failover (switching to a backup database if the primary one fails), and load balancing (distributing requests evenly across multiple databases).

2. Transaction Management: Middleware plays a critical role in transaction management, particularly for transactions that span multiple databases or other resources. It can handle tasks like initiating, committing, and rolling back transactions, ensuring consistency (all parts of a transaction are completed or none are), and managing distributed transactions (transactions that span across multiple databases).

3. Data Translation and Mapping: Middleware often includes functionality to translate data between different formats, such as converting XML or JSON data into a format suitable for a relational database, and vice versa. It may also provide Object-Relational Mapping (ORM) capabilities, which enable developers to interact with databases using object-oriented programming languages, without needing to write SQL.

4. Data Caching: Middleware can also provide data caching

services, temporarily storing frequently accessed data closer to the application to reduce database load and improve performance.

5. Security: Middleware assists in implementing security measures such as authentication and encryption, ensuring that only authorized applications can access and manipulate the data.

In conclusion, middleware acts as the bridge between applications and databases, providing essential services that enable smooth, efficient, and secure interactions, which are particularly critical in a transaction processing environment where data integrity, consistency, and performance are paramount.

10.5 Middleware and Mainframe Programming Languages

MIDDLEWARE IN A MAINFRAME environment interfaces with mainframe programming languages to facilitate the execution of operations and handle transactions. This interaction is critical for a number of reasons:

1. Facilitating Communication: Middleware often provides a communication interface or an Application Programming Interface (API) that programming languages can use to communicate with other software components. This interface simplifies the communication process, allowing developers to focus on the logic of their applications rather than the specifics of inter-process communication.

2. Transaction Management: Middleware provides services for managing transactions, including features like beginning, committing, or rolling back a transaction. Programming languages can interface with middleware to leverage these features, ensuring that all the steps in a transaction are completed successfully or none of them are, maintaining the ACID properties (Atomicity, Consistency, Isolation, Durability).

3. Resource Pooling: Middleware often manages resources like database connections or messaging queues. Programming languages can use the middleware's API to access these pooled resources, improving application efficiency and scalability.

4. Data Mapping: Middleware can provide data mapping services, translating between the data structures used by a database and the data structures used by a programming language. This simplifies the process of writing and reading

data from a database.

5. Error Handling: Middleware can also assist with error handling. For instance, if an error occurs during a database operation, the middleware can catch that error, log it, and then relay it to the application in a format that's easy for the application to interpret.

Commonly used mainframe programming languages like COBOL, Java, and PL/I, can interact with middleware to leverage these services, allowing developers to write efficient, robust, and scalable applications for transaction processing.

10.6 Middleware Tools and Utilities

THIS SECTION OF THE chapter discusses some of the most commonly used tools and utilities when working with middleware in the context of mainframe transaction processing.

1. Monitoring Tools: Middleware often includes monitoring tools or is compatible with third-party monitoring tools that can be used to track the performance of middleware components, identify potential issues, and monitor transaction processes. These tools can provide insights into key metrics like transaction speed, system load, or error rates.

2. Testing and Debugging Tools: There are various tools available that can help developers test and debug their applications in a middleware environment. These can include automated testing frameworks, logging tools, and debugging utilities that can trace transaction flow, simulate various scenarios, and analyze system behavior to help locate and fix issues.

3. Development and Deployment Tools: Middleware often comes with integrated development environments (IDEs) or is compatible with third-party IDEs, which developers can use to write and deploy their applications. These tools can assist with code editing, version control, build automation, and the deployment of applications.

4. Data Mapping Tools: In a middleware context, data mapping tools are often used to map data between different formats or structures. This is particularly important when dealing with diverse data sources or targets in transaction processing.

5. Security Tools: Middleware systems often include security

tools or can integrate with third-party security solutions to help protect data and ensure the integrity of transactions. These tools can manage authentication, authorization, encryption, and other aspects of security.

6. Administration and Configuration Tools: These tools help system administrators manage and configure middleware components. They can assist with tasks like resource allocation, load balancing, failover, backup and restore operations, and more.

Each of these tools and utilities play a critical role in helping developers and administrators create, manage, and optimize middleware systems for mainframe transaction processing.

10.7 Middleware in the Modern Mainframe World

IN THIS PART OF THE chapter, we discuss the evolution and current trends of middleware in modern mainframe environments. As the world of mainframe computing has evolved, so has the role and sophistication of middleware technologies. They have had to adapt to changes such as the rise of cloud computing, the increasing need for distributed systems, and the shift towards service-oriented architectures (SOA).

1. Cloud Computing: Cloud computing offers scalability, flexibility, and cost-efficiency, characteristics that have attracted many businesses to move their mainframe workloads to the cloud. In this scenario, middleware plays an integral role in integrating cloud-based resources with existing mainframe applications. This allows for seamless communication and data transfer between cloud services and mainframe systems. In addition, middleware often provides capabilities for handling the security, transaction integrity, and performance concerns that come with the cloud.

2. Distributed Systems: In the age of global business operations, distributed systems have become more commonplace. Middleware in these environments ensures communication and data consistency across various systems, enabling them to function as a single, unified system. This includes supporting distributed transactions, where a single transaction might involve changes to multiple resources, potentially distributed across different physical locations.

3. Service-Oriented Architectures (SOA): In a service-

oriented architecture, applications are designed as a collection of services that communicate with each other. Middleware supports this architecture by providing communication and message routing capabilities between services, irrespective of where those services are hosted. Middleware helps in managing transactions across multiple services, ensuring consistency and reliability.

4. Microservices and Containers: The recent trend towards microservices and containerization has influenced the way middleware is designed and used. Middleware provides the necessary infrastructure for microservices to communicate and interact with each other and with the mainframe. This includes service discovery, load balancing, data transformation, and transaction management.

5. Integration with Modern Programming Languages and Frameworks: Modern middleware solutions are also evolving to support a wide range of programming languages and development frameworks. This allows developers to use the most appropriate language and tools for the job at hand, while still leveraging the robust transaction processing capabilities of the mainframe.

In conclusion, middleware remains a vital component in mainframe transaction processing, and it continues to evolve and adapt to meet the needs of modern mainframe environments. The demand for high-performance, reliable, and secure transaction processing in these complex environments ensures that middleware will continue to be a critical part of the mainframe ecosystem.

10.8 Conclusion

THIS CONCLUDING SECTION summarizes the key points discussed in this chapter and reflects on the essential role of middleware in mainframe transaction processing.

The chapter started with an introduction to the concept of middleware, outlining its critical role in managing interactions between different software components in a mainframe environment. Middleware acts as a glue that holds together various parts of a system, managing communication, data exchange, and ensuring coordination among the diverse elements of the mainframe ecosystem.

Next, we examined different types of middleware used in mainframe environments. These include message-oriented middleware, application servers, and database access middleware. Each type serves a unique function and is chosen based on the requirements of the specific application or system setup.

We further explored the integral role of middleware in transaction processing. Middleware manages transactions across multiple disparate systems, ensuring consistency and reliability while also minimizing complexity for the application developer.

The interaction between middleware and databases was discussed, illustrating how middleware aids in database connectivity, transaction management, and data translation. Middleware serves as an abstraction layer, allowing applications to interact with databases without needing to understand the specifics of the database systems.

Similarly, the relationship between middleware and mainframe programming languages was discussed. Middleware provides interfaces that allow various programming languages to execute operations and handle transactions, thereby broadening the range of tools available for mainframe developers.

The chapter also walked through some common tools and utilities that are used in conjunction with middleware for mainframe transaction processing, providing a more practical understanding of middleware utilization.

Finally, we looked at how middleware is evolving to meet the demands of modern mainframe environments. The impact of cloud computing, distributed systems, and service-oriented architectures on middleware was discussed, emphasizing how middleware continues to adapt and remain relevant in the face of these changes.

In conclusion, middleware is a fundamental component in mainframe transaction processing. Its role as a facilitator for communication, transaction management, and integration is crucial in ensuring the smooth and efficient operation of mainframe systems. As the technology landscape continues to evolve, middleware is expected to continue adapting to meet new challenges and requirements. Understanding middleware's functionalities and its interactions with other mainframe components is, therefore, vital for anyone involved in mainframe transaction processing.

Part IV: The Architecture and Lifecycle of Mainframe Transaction Processing

———

In Part IV of the book, we delve into the architecture and lifecycle of mainframe transaction processing. This section aims to provide an in-depth understanding of how transactions are processed in mainframes, from inception to completion, along with a comprehensive view of the architectural components that underpin this process. Additionally, we examine the vital subject of security in mainframe transaction processing.

Chapter 11: The Architecture of Mainframe Transaction Processing: This chapter provides a detailed overview of the architectural components that facilitate transaction processing in a mainframe environment. From hardware and operating systems to databases, middleware, and programming languages, each aspect is explored in depth to help the reader grasp the structure of mainframe transaction processing systems.

Chapter 12: The Transaction Processing Lifecycle: In this chapter, we take a closer look at the life cycle of a transaction in a mainframe system, tracing its path from the initiation of a request, through processing and database interaction, to final completion. This lifecycle perspective offers crucial insights into the functionality and operation of mainframe transaction processing.

Chapter 13: Security in Mainframe Transaction Processing: This final chapter underlines the importance of security in mainframe transaction processing. Given the critical and sensitive nature of the data handled by mainframes, robust security measures are paramount. This chapter explores the various security measures, mechanisms, and best practices used to protect data and ensure the integrity and confidentiality of transactions.

Chapter 11: The Architecture of Mainframe Transaction Processing

———

Chapter 11 focuses on the architecture of mainframe transaction processing. The chapter provides a detailed view of the interplay between various hardware and software components that facilitate transaction processing in a mainframe environment.

Here are the sections of Chapter 11:

11.1 Introduction to Mainframe Transaction Processing Architecture: This section provides an overview of the architecture of mainframe transaction processing, discussing its significance and main features.

11.2 Mainframe Hardware in Transaction Processing: Here we explore the role of mainframe hardware in transaction processing, including processors, storage devices, and networking components.

11.3 Operating Systems in Transaction Processing: This part focuses on the role of operating systems in transaction processing, explaining their interaction with hardware and other software components.

11.4 Databases in Transaction Processing: This section examines the crucial role of databases in transaction processing, including hierarchical, relational, and modern NoSQL databases.

11.5 Middleware in Transaction Processing: An overview of the role of middleware in coordinating and facilitating interaction between various software components in transaction processing.

11.6 Programming Languages in Transaction Processing: Here we discuss the role of programming languages, from traditional ones like COBOL and PL/I to modern ones like Java and Python, in developing transaction processing applications.

11.7 Security Architecture in Transaction Processing: A look at the security measures and mechanisms integrated into the architecture to protect data and transactions.

11.8 The Modern Mainframe Transaction Processing Architecture: This part discusses the evolution of mainframe transaction processing architecture to adapt to modern requirements such as distributed systems, cloud computing, and service-oriented architectures.

11.9 Conclusion: A summary of the key points discussed in the chapter, reflecting on the importance of understanding the architecture of mainframe transaction processing.

11.1 Introduction to Mainframe Transaction Processing Architecture

THE ARCHITECTURE OF mainframe transaction processing forms the backbone of many industries, handling vast volumes of transactions efficiently and securely. It is designed to provide high performance, reliability, and availability, which are crucial in sectors such as finance, healthcare, and government, among others. This section sets the stage by providing an overview of this architecture, explaining its significance, and describing its main features.

Here are some of the main points discussed in this section:

- Role and Importance: The discussion begins with the role and importance of mainframe transaction processing architecture. It is critical in ensuring efficient processing of transactions, maintaining data integrity, managing concurrency, and providing fault tolerance and recovery mechanisms.
- Components: The section also introduces the primary components involved in transaction processing, including mainframe hardware, operating systems, middleware, databases, and programming languages. Each of these plays a crucial role in the overall process.
- Mainframe Strengths: The inherent strengths of the mainframe, such as robustness, reliability, and scalability, are highlighted as key reasons behind their enduring relevance in transaction processing.
- Modern Relevance: The section underscores the modern relevance of mainframes, dispelling the notion that they are outdated or obsolete. Despite advances in other forms of computing, mainframes continue to be a staple in

industries that need to process large volumes of
transactions quickly and securely.

Overall, the introduction provides a high-level view of mainframe
transaction processing architecture, paving the way for more detailed
discussions in the following sections.

11.2 Mainframe Hardware in Transaction Processing

THIS SECTION DELVES into the role that mainframe hardware plays in transaction processing. In a mainframe environment, the hardware is designed and optimized for high-throughput, reliable transaction processing. The section discusses major hardware components such as processors, storage devices, and networking components.

- Processors: The mainframe's processors, also known as central processing units (CPUs), are responsible for executing instructions of computer programs involved in transaction processing. Modern mainframes are equipped with powerful multi-core processors which can handle many threads simultaneously, allowing for the processing of a high volume of transactions.
- Storage Devices: Data involved in transaction processing is stored on various storage devices in a mainframe. These include both primary storage (such as RAM for fast, temporary storage of data) and secondary storage (such as hard disk drives or solid-state drives for long-term data storage). Mainframes are designed to handle vast amounts of data, thus they have large capacities for data storage.
- Networking Components: These are crucial in a mainframe environment as they enable connectivity between the mainframe and other systems, whether they're other mainframes, servers, or end-user devices. They also enable connectivity between the mainframe and its storage devices. Networking components handle the communication protocols and data transmission, ensuring that data is exchanged quickly, reliably, and securely.

The mainframe's hardware is crucial in transaction processing as it directly influences the system's performance, reliability, and capability in handling high transaction volumes. Mainframe hardware is purpose-built and fine-tuned to handle transaction processing workloads, making it a key factor in the high performance of mainframes in these tasks.

11.3 Operating Systems in Transaction Processing

THIS SECTION OF THE chapter will provide insight into the role of operating systems in mainframe transaction processing. Operating systems are a crucial component of any computing environment, as they manage hardware resources and provide services for software applications.

In the context of mainframe transaction processing, the operating system takes on a vital role for the following reasons:

- Resource Allocation: One of the key responsibilities of an operating system is to manage the computer's resources, which include the CPU, memory, storage devices, and input/output devices. The operating system allocates these resources to various processes and applications. In transaction processing, this could mean assigning processing power to different transactions based on their priority or order of arrival.

- Process Management: In transaction processing, multiple transactions can be processed simultaneously. The operating system manages these concurrent processes, ensuring that each transaction is correctly executed and completed without interfering with others. This includes scheduling processes, creating and terminating processes, and handling process synchronization and inter-process communication.

- Memory Management: The operating system is responsible for managing the computer's memory. This involves keeping track of each byte in the system's memory, deciding which processes will receive memory, and when they will receive it. In transaction processing, the operating system ensures that each transaction has the necessary memory space to be processed efficiently.

- File System Management: Mainframe transaction processing involves a lot of data that needs to be stored and retrieved from the system's storage devices. The operating system manages the file system, controlling how data is read and written, ensuring data integrity and providing fast access to databases.

- Security: The operating system also provides security mechanisms to protect data and system resources. This is especially important in transaction processing, where sensitive data needs to be protected from unauthorized access and manipulation.

Common operating systems used in mainframes include z/OS, z/VSE, and z/VM from IBM. These operating systems are specifically designed for mainframe architecture and are optimized for high-volume, high-speed transaction processing.

11.4 Databases in Transaction Processing

IN THIS SECTION, WE focus on the role of databases in the context of mainframe transaction processing. Databases are a critical component because they store and manage the data that is involved in transactions.

Here are the key points this section would likely cover:

- The role of databases: Transactions involve retrieving, adding, updating, or deleting data. All of this data is stored in databases. As such, databases are at the heart of any transaction processing system. They are responsible for storing transaction data persistently and making it available for processing as needed.
- Hierarchical databases: This type of database, represented by systems like IBM's Information Management System (IMS), organizes data in a tree-like model, where each piece of data has one parent node and zero or more child nodes. This structure is particularly useful for applications where there is a one-to-many relationship between records, like in banking or telecommunication systems.
- Relational databases: These databases, represented by systems like IBM's DB2, organize data into tables of rows and columns, with each row representing a record and each column representing a field in the record. They support complex queries and are widely used due to their flexibility and ease of use.
- Modern NoSQL databases: NoSQL databases are a recent development designed to address the limitations of relational databases, particularly regarding scalability and flexibility. NoSQL databases, like MongoDB and

Cassandra, offer a variety of data models, including key-value, document, column-family, and graph formats. NoSQL databases are increasingly being adopted in mainframe environments to handle unstructured data and provide flexible schemas for evolving data requirements.

- Database Management Systems (DBMS): A DBMS is software that interacts with users, other applications, and the database itself to capture and analyze data. The DBMS manages three important things: the data, the database engine, and the database schema. In the context of transaction processing, the DBMS plays a crucial role in ensuring data consistency and integrity.
- Transaction management in databases: The database systems play a crucial role in managing transactions. They enforce the ACID properties (Atomicity, Consistency, Isolation, Durability) to ensure reliable processing. This includes locking resources during a transaction, logging changes for potential rollbacks or recovery, and ensuring the changes of a transaction are saved permanently upon completion.

The choice of a database system depends on the specific requirements of the application, including the nature of the data, the volume of transactions, and the needed performance and reliability characteristics.

11.5 Middleware in Transaction Processing

IN THIS SECTION, WE examine the role of middleware in the context of mainframe transaction processing. Middleware is essentially the glue that binds together various disparate systems and software components in a larger network, making it possible for them to communicate and work together effectively. It lies between the operating system and the applications on each side of a distributed computer network. Typically, it supports complex, distributed business software applications.

Here are the key points this section would likely cover:

- Role of Middleware: Middleware serves as a bridge between applications and other software components or databases. It enables communication and data management, so different applications can work together. In the context of mainframe transaction processing, middleware is crucial for handling and orchestrating numerous simultaneous transactions that may involve multiple databases or software applications.
- Types of Middleware: There are several types of middleware used in mainframe transaction processing, including:
    - Message-Oriented Middleware (MOM): This facilitates communication between distributed systems through message queues. This allows for asynchronous communication, where the sender and receiver do not need to interact with the message queue at the same time. Examples include IBM's MQ series.
    - Transaction Processing Monitors (TPMs): They

handle transaction management for the system, including facilitating communication, maintaining security, and ensuring data integrity during transactions. Examples include IBM's CICS and IMS systems.

○ Database Access Middleware: This enables applications to interact with databases. It provides an abstraction layer that allows developers to perform database operations without needing to know the specifics of each database's protocol.

- Middleware and Transactions: In transaction processing, middleware can provide several critical services, including routing, data transformation, and transaction management. It may also handle tasks such as load balancing, failover, and transaction monitoring to ensure that all transactions are processed reliably and efficiently.

- Middleware in Modern Mainframes: As mainframe systems become increasingly interconnected and as the demand for real-time data access grows, the role of middleware continues to expand. Middleware solutions are continually evolving to support new communication protocols, improved performance, and enhanced security measures.

In summary, middleware plays a crucial role in mainframe transaction processing, enabling different software components to work together seamlessly and efficiently. It provides a unified approach to managing and coordinating transactions across diverse and distributed environments.

11.6 Programming Languages in Transaction Processing

IN THIS SECTION, WE delve into the role of programming languages in mainframe transaction processing. The choice of programming language can have a significant impact on the performance, reliability, and ease of development of transaction processing applications.

Here are the key points this section would likely cover:

- Traditional Languages: Traditional languages such as COBOL and PL/I have been the bedrock of mainframe transaction processing for many years. These languages were designed with business applications in mind and are known for their robustness and reliability. They have a rich set of features for handling data, and their syntax is highly readable, making it easier to maintain and modify code.
    - COBOL: The Common Business-Oriented Language, developed in the late 1950s, was designed for business data processing needs and has been a cornerstone in the mainframe world. COBOL excels in processing large volumes of data, making it an ideal choice for transaction processing.
    - PL/I: Programming Language One, another traditional language used in mainframes, incorporates features from both COBOL (business applications) and Fortran (scientific computation). It is often used for complex scientific applications that involve large-scale transaction processing.

- Java on Mainframes: Java has gained popularity in the mainframe environment due to its platform-independent nature and robust feature set. It has a range of libraries and frameworks that facilitate the development of transaction processing applications. It's particularly well-suited for building web-based applications, providing services like multi-threading, networking, and security protocols.
- Modern Languages: Languages such as Python and Swift have begun to find a place in the mainframe environment. These languages, while not traditionally associated with mainframes, offer benefits such as rapid development and a large ecosystem of libraries and frameworks. They are often used in conjunction with traditional languages to build modern, web-based interfaces to mainframe applications.
- Language Selection: The choice of programming language depends on several factors, including the specific requirements of the transaction processing application, the skills of the development team, and the existing software infrastructure. Different languages have different strengths and can be used together to build robust and efficient transaction processing systems.

In conclusion, programming languages play a critical role in mainframe transaction processing. They provide the tools necessary for developers to create applications that can handle large volumes of transactions efficiently and reliably. From traditional languages like COBOL and PL/I to modern ones like Java and Python, each language has a role to play in the evolving landscape of mainframe transaction processing.

11.7 Security Architecture in Transaction Processing

IN THIS SECTION, WE'LL examine the various security measures and mechanisms that are integrated into the architecture of mainframe transaction processing to protect data and transactions.

Key topics covered in this section might include:

- Data Security: Protecting data is a primary concern in transaction processing. Measures to ensure data security can include encryption (both at rest and in transit), masking and redaction (for sensitive data), secure logging and monitoring, and hardened database configurations.
- User Authentication and Authorization: Mainframe systems often employ robust user authentication mechanisms, such as multi-factor authentication, to verify the identity of users before they can access the system. Once authenticated, authorization protocols ensure that users can only access and perform operations that they are permitted to do.
- Transaction Integrity: Mechanisms are put in place to ensure the ACID (Atomicity, Consistency, Isolation, Durability) properties of transactions. This involves using techniques like two-phase commit and compensating transactions, which help ensure that even in the event of system failures, transaction integrity is maintained.
- Network Security: Since mainframe systems often interact with a variety of other systems over networks, network security is a crucial aspect. This can include firewalls, secure communication protocols like TLS, intrusion detection systems (IDS), and intrusion prevention systems (IPS).

- Auditing and Compliance: Mainframe transaction processing systems typically have extensive auditing capabilities to track who did what and when. This is particularly important in regulated industries, where compliance with standards like PCI-DSS, HIPAA, and GDPR is required.
- Security Standards and Best Practices: Security in mainframe transaction processing is typically guided by industry standards and best practices. This can include standards like the ISO 27000 series for information security management, as well as best practices from industry groups like the Cloud Security Alliance (CSA) or the Center for Internet Security (CIS).

In conclusion, security is an integral part of the architecture of mainframe transaction processing. Given the high stakes involved – transaction processing systems often handle highly sensitive data and mission-critical operations – it's no surprise that these systems are designed with security at their core. From data encryption to user authentication, network protections to auditing capabilities, every aspect of the system is designed to ensure the highest possible level of security.

11.8 The Modern Mainframe Transaction Processing Architecture

IN THIS SECTION, WE'LL delve into the evolution of the mainframe transaction processing architecture to adapt to modern requirements such as distributed systems, cloud computing, and service-oriented architectures.

Over the past few decades, the computing landscape has seen significant changes. The rise of distributed computing, the Internet, cloud-based solutions, and the adoption of service-oriented architectures have revolutionized how businesses and organizations operate. These developments have necessitated changes in the architecture of mainframe transaction processing systems to ensure they remain efficient, reliable, and relevant.

Distributed Systems: Distributed systems allow computing tasks to be divided among several computers rather than relying on a single machine. Mainframes have adapted to this environment by supporting distributed transaction processing. This means that a single transaction can involve multiple systems, possibly located in different geographical locations. Distributed transactions are coordinated to ensure ACID properties are maintained across all involved systems.

Cloud Computing: The adoption of cloud computing has been transformative in the IT world. Mainframes have evolved to integrate with the cloud in several ways. Hybrid cloud architectures are now common, where part of the processing happens on a mainframe and part happens in a public or private cloud environment. Additionally, virtualization technologies allow mainframes to host multiple virtual machines (VMs), effectively turning them into private clouds.

Service-Oriented Architectures (SOA): SOA is a software design approach where applications are built based on services – self-contained units of functionality that communicate with each other via standard interfaces and protocols. Mainframes have embraced this concept, and many mainframe applications are now built or adapted to work within SOA environments. For example, traditional mainframe applications may be wrapped in a service layer that exposes their functionality via web services, which can be easily consumed by other applications, potentially running on entirely different platforms.

Microservices and Containers: Microservices architecture, where an application is built as a collection of small, independent services, is a further evolution of SOA. Coupled with container technologies like Docker and orchestration tools like Kubernetes, this approach is gaining popularity due to its scalability and flexibility benefits. Although these are traditionally associated with distributed, cloud-native applications, mainframe transaction processing systems are also adopting these concepts. Mainframe environments now often support running containerized workloads, and some traditional mainframe applications are being refactored into microservices.

In summary, the architecture of mainframe transaction processing systems has evolved significantly to keep pace with modern computing trends. While preserving their core strengths – high performance, reliability, and security – mainframes have adapted to work effectively in distributed, cloud-based, and service-oriented environments, demonstrating their continued relevance in the modern IT landscape.

11.9 Conclusion

THE CONCLUDING SECTION of this chapter serves to summarize and reinforce the key concepts that have been discussed, bringing together the various components that comprise mainframe transaction processing architecture and their roles.

The architecture of mainframe transaction processing is complex and multi-layered, involving multiple hardware and software components. Each part of this architecture plays a unique role in supporting high-volume, rapid transaction processing:

1. Mainframe Hardware: The power and reliability of mainframe hardware are fundamental to transaction processing. Components like processors, storage devices, and networking hardware are designed to deliver high performance and durability, ensuring transactions are processed rapidly and reliably.

2. Operating Systems: Mainframe operating systems, like z/OS, provide an essential layer of abstraction between the hardware and software. They manage resources, provide services to applications, and ensure efficient execution of transactions.

3. Databases: Databases hold the data that is the focus of transaction processing. Different types of databases, including hierarchical, relational, and NoSQL databases, can be used in mainframes, each with its unique strengths and use cases.

4. Middleware: Middleware facilitates interaction between various software components involved in transaction processing. It can handle tasks like message routing, transaction coordination, and database connectivity.

5. Programming Languages: A variety of programming languages, both traditional and modern, are used in mainframe transaction processing. These languages, including COBOL, PL/I, Java, and Python, allow developers to implement business logic and interact with other components of the system.

6. Security Architecture: Security is a fundamental aspect of mainframe transaction processing. Various security mechanisms are integrated into the system architecture to ensure the confidentiality, integrity, and availability of data and transactions.

The modern mainframe architecture has evolved significantly to adapt to contemporary IT paradigms such as distributed systems, cloud computing, and service-oriented architectures. Despite these adaptations, the core strength of mainframes - their ability to process large volumes of transactions reliably and efficiently - remains unchanged.

Understanding the architecture of mainframe transaction processing is key to appreciating its strengths, capabilities, and adaptability to the modern IT landscape. As we continue to see evolution in the IT field, mainframes have demonstrated their ability to adapt and continue to play a critical role in enterprise computing.

Chapter 12: The Transaction Processing Lifecycle

———

This chapter provides a comprehensive look at the lifecycle of a transaction within a mainframe environment. From the initiation of a transaction to its final completion or rollback in case of errors, this lifecycle is explored in detail to provide a clear understanding of the processes involved in mainframe transaction processing.

Here are the main sections of the chapter:

12.1 Introduction to the Transaction Processing Lifecycle: This section offers a general overview of the transaction processing lifecycle, explaining what it is, why it's essential, and the steps generally involved.

12.2 Initiating a Transaction: Here, the process of initiating a transaction in a mainframe environment is discussed. This includes client requests, system responses, and the roles various components play in starting a transaction.

12.3 Transaction Processing and Coordination: This part delves into the coordination aspects of transaction processing, detailing how different system components work together to execute and monitor transactions.

12.4 Transaction Isolation and Consistency: In this section, we explore how mainframe systems maintain isolation and consistency during transaction processing.

This includes discussions on ACID properties, locking mechanisms, and isolation levels.

12.5 Error Handling and Recovery in Transaction Processing: This part of the chapter discusses how mainframe systems handle errors during transaction processing and the measures put in place for recovery.

12.6 Transaction Completion and Commitment: Here, the final stages of transaction processing are covered, including successful completion, data commitment, and transaction termination.

12.7 Monitoring and Tuning the Transaction Processing Lifecycle: This section looks at the tools and methodologies for monitoring transaction processing and strategies for performance tuning.

12.8 The Transaction Processing Lifecycle in the Modern Mainframe World: This part explores how the transaction processing lifecycle fits into the modern mainframe landscape and how it's evolved over time to cater to newer paradigms like distributed transactions.

12.9 Conclusion: The chapter concludes with a summary of the key points discussed, reflecting on the significance of understanding the transaction processing lifecycle in a mainframe environment.

12.1 Introduction to the Transaction Processing Lifecycle

THE TRANSACTION PROCESSING lifecycle refers to the sequence of steps that a transaction undergoes from initiation to completion within a mainframe system. In simple terms, a transaction is a logical unit of work that may comprise multiple related operations, all of which must succeed for the transaction to be considered successful.

Understanding the transaction processing lifecycle is crucial for several reasons:

1. Data Consistency: The lifecycle is designed to ensure data consistency, that is, to maintain the integrity of data during updates. It ensures that even in the event of a system failure, transactions can be rolled back or replayed to achieve a consistent state.
2. Concurrency Control: The lifecycle also helps manage concurrent transactions, allowing multiple users to access and modify data simultaneously without conflict.
3. Recovery and Fault Tolerance: The steps in the transaction processing lifecycle provide mechanisms for error detection, logging, and recovery, making the system resilient to hardware and software failures.
4. Performance Optimization: Understanding the lifecycle can guide performance optimization efforts. For instance, adjusting transaction isolation levels or lock granularity can improve throughput and response times.

The steps generally involved in the transaction processing lifecycle include:

1. Initiation: The transaction begins, typically in response to a user request.
2. Processing: The transaction is executed, involving one or more operations such as reads, writes, updates, or deletes on the database.
3. Commitment: If all operations succeed, the transaction is committed, and all changes are permanently applied to the database.
4. Termination: The transaction ends, and resources used during the transaction are released.

In case of errors or failures during the processing stage, the transaction may be rolled back instead of committed, reversing any changes made during the transaction. After a rollback, the transaction also ends, and resources are released.

Throughout this chapter, we will be exploring these steps and related concepts in greater detail.

12.2 Initiating a Transaction

INITIATING A TRANSACTION in a mainframe environment is the first step in the transaction processing lifecycle and is typically triggered by a client request. These client requests can be user-initiated actions from a front-end application, batch jobs, API calls, or other types of system events.

The process involves several steps and components:

1. Client Request: The transaction begins with a client request. This can take many forms such as a user entering data into a form on a web interface, an automated system sending an API request, a batch process starting a set of jobs, or a timed event triggering a specific action.
2. Request Handling: The request is then handled by a middleware layer, which is responsible for managing communication between the client and the mainframe. The middleware translates the client's request into a format that can be processed by the mainframe.
3. Routing: The translated request is then routed to the appropriate system component. This could be a particular program or process that handles these types of requests. Transaction monitors, such as CICS or IMS, can facilitate this routing process based on the transaction code or identifier included in the request.
4. Transaction Initialization: Once the request is received by the appropriate program or process, it initiates the transaction. It's important to note that a transaction, in this context, is not just the client's request, but the entire sequence of operations needed to fulfill that request. These operations could involve fetching, updating, inserting, or

deleting data from a database.

5. Resource Allocation: As part of the initialization process, the system also allocates the resources needed to complete the transaction. This could include setting up memory space for the transaction, establishing database connections, or locking resources to prevent conflicts with other concurrent transactions.

Throughout this process, various components of the mainframe environment work together to initiate the transaction, ensuring that it's correctly routed and that all necessary resources are prepared. In the following sections, we will delve into the subsequent steps in the transaction processing lifecycle.

12.3 Transaction Processing and Coordination

TRANSACTION PROCESSING and coordination form the heart of the transaction processing lifecycle. After the transaction initiation stage, the system must then execute and coordinate the different steps of the transaction to ensure accurate and consistent outcomes.

1. Execution: The transaction's instructions are executed, which typically involve operations on the database such as reads, writes, updates, or deletes. The execution is managed by a combination of transaction processing systems like CICS or IMS and the DBMS (Database Management System) like DB2 or IMS DB. The exact operations and their order will depend on the specifics of the transaction.

2. Coordination: The coordination aspect ensures that all components involved in the transaction are working together seamlessly. This includes coordinating with the DBMS to lock and unlock database resources, ensuring the right sequence of operations, and managing communication between different parts of the system or different systems.

3. Monitoring: Transaction processing systems also monitor the progress of the transaction. They keep track of the state of the transaction and all the resources it's interacting with. This is important for ensuring the consistency and reliability of the system.

4. Synchronization: Transactions often require the system to coordinate multiple operations that need to happen in a certain order. This could involve operations on multiple records in a database or interactions between multiple systems. Synchronization mechanisms, such as locking and

latching, are used to ensure that operations occur in the correct order and that they don't interfere with each other.

5. Error Handling: If errors occur during transaction execution, such as data conflicts or system failures, the transaction processing system must handle these gracefully. This might involve rolling back the transaction to its initial state, logging the error for future investigation, and triggering any necessary error recovery processes.

The coordination of transaction processing ensures that transactions are executed accurately and efficiently, maintaining the system's integrity and reliability. This complexity is managed by the sophisticated transaction processing systems and middleware that underpin mainframe environments.

12.4 Transaction Isolation and Consistency

TRANSACTION ISOLATION and Consistency are vital attributes in any transaction processing system. These features enable the system to manage multiple transactions simultaneously without compromising data integrity.

1. ACID Properties: ACID stands for Atomicity, Consistency, Isolation, and Durability, which are fundamental properties of reliable transaction processing.
   ◦ Atomicity ensures that a transaction is treated as a single, indivisible operation, which either fully completes or fails entirely, without leaving the system in an intermediate state.
   ◦ Consistency ensures that transactions bring the system from one valid state to another, preserving the rules of the databases (such as unique keys or data types).
   ◦ Isolation means that the execution of concurrent transactions results in a system state that would be obtained if transactions were executed serially, i.e., one after the other.
   ◦ Durability ensures that once a transaction has been committed, it will remain committed even in the case of a system failure.
2. Locking Mechanisms: These are tools that manage the simultaneous access of shared resources. Locks can be on various levels, such as rows, tables, or databases, and can be shared (for read access) or exclusive (for write access). The choice of lock granularity and type can greatly influence the system's performance and concurrency level.
3. Isolation Levels: Isolation levels are a way to define the

degree of isolation between transactions. Higher isolation levels provide greater data consistency but can reduce system performance due to more extensive locking mechanisms. Mainframe systems offer different isolation levels, such as Read Uncommitted, Read Committed, Repeatable Read, and Serializable, to provide a balance between data integrity and system performance.

4. Consistency Checks: These are procedures to ensure the integrity of the data. For example, if a transaction tries to violate a database's rules (like inserting a duplicate key or violating a foreign key constraint), the system must detect this and abort the transaction.

Maintaining transaction isolation and consistency is a critical aspect of transaction processing on mainframes. Mainframes excel at this due to their powerful transaction processing systems and sophisticated concurrency control mechanisms.

12.5 Error Handling and Recovery in Transaction Processing

ERROR HANDLING AND Recovery are two critical aspects of transaction processing. They ensure that the system remains reliable and stable, even in the face of unexpected conditions or failures.

1. Error Handling: During transaction processing, various errors can occur, such as system errors, hardware faults, application errors, or network issues. The mainframe system has robust error handling mechanisms to manage these situations effectively. These may include:

    ◦ Exception Handling: When an error occurs during the execution of a transaction, the system throws an exception. The programming languages used in mainframes have constructs to catch and handle these exceptions, ensuring that the transaction processing does not halt abruptly.

    ◦ Error Logging: Information about the errors encountered during transaction processing is often logged in an error log. This includes error codes, error messages, and other diagnostic information that can be used for troubleshooting and resolution of the issues.

    ◦ Error Notification: The system may provide real-time alerts or notifications to administrators or operators when significant errors occur. This allows for immediate attention and action to resolve the issue.

2. Recovery: When a system or application error occurs, it is crucial to restore the system to a consistent state and resume normal operation as quickly as possible. Recovery

mechanisms in mainframe transaction processing systems include:

- Transaction Rollback: If a transaction cannot be completed due to an error, the changes made by the transaction need to be undone to preserve data integrity. This is achieved by rolling back the transaction, which involves reversing the actions of the transaction to bring the system back to its state before the transaction started.

- Journaling and Checkpointing: These techniques are used to recover transactions in the event of a system failure. Journaling involves keeping a log of all changes made by transactions. Checkpointing is a mechanism where the state of the system is saved periodically. In the event of a failure, the system can be restored to the most recent checkpoint, and the transactions since that checkpoint can be redone using the journal.

- Backup and Restore: Regular backups of databases are maintained, which can be used to restore the system to a consistent state in case of severe failures.

Error handling and recovery are fundamental aspects of mainframe transaction processing systems, contributing to their reputation for high reliability and robustness.

12.6 Transaction Completion and Commitment

TRANSACTION COMPLETION and Commitment mark the final stages in the transaction processing lifecycle in a mainframe system. The section can be further divided into the following parts:

1. Successful Completion: Once all the operations of a transaction have been executed without errors, the transaction is said to have successfully completed. However, successful completion doesn't immediately make the changes to the database permanent. These changes are held in a temporary buffer or workspace until they can be committed to the database.
2. Data Commitment: Commitment is the process of making the changes of a transaction permanent. When a transaction is committed, all changes it made in the buffer or workspace are written to the database. Once committed, these changes can't be rolled back or undone. It's the responsibility of the transaction management system to decide the optimal time to commit a transaction, which often involves considerations for concurrency, system performance, and ACID properties.
3. Transaction Termination: Following the commitment, the transaction is terminated. Termination marks the end of the transaction's lifecycle. All resources that were allocated to the transaction, such as memory, locks, or CPU, are released for use by other transactions. If there were any errors during the transaction, and it couldn't be completed successfully, it's rolled back, and the transaction is also terminated.
4. Transaction Logging: All transaction activities, including

commitment and termination, are logged in a transaction log. The log contains a record of all committed and terminated transactions, which can be used for debugging, auditing, and recovery purposes.

This understanding of the transaction completion and commitment process is crucial, as it ensures data consistency and reliability in a mainframe environment. This process, while invisible to end-users, is a cornerstone of the robustness and reliability of mainframe transaction processing systems.

12.7 Monitoring and Tuning the Transaction Processing Lifecycle

MONITORING AND TUNING are critical activities in the management of the transaction processing lifecycle in a mainframe environment. Here's a detailed breakdown of this section:

1. Monitoring Transaction Processing: Monitoring is the process of observing and checking the progress or quality of something over a period of time. In the context of transaction processing, monitoring involves keeping an eye on system performance, transaction execution times, resource usage, error rates, and system health metrics. Monitoring tools, which provide real-time or near-real-time information about these parameters, are essential for effective transaction processing management. They help system administrators identify potential bottlenecks, troubleshoot problems, and plan for capacity upgrades.

2. Tuning Transaction Processing: Tuning refers to the process of adjusting the parameters of a system to improve its performance. In transaction processing, this could involve tweaking database parameters (like memory allocation, index structures, or query optimization), adjusting system settings (like process scheduling or priority), or optimizing application code. The goal is to minimize response time, maximize throughput, and generally make the system as efficient as possible.

3. Use of Tools: Several tools are available to help with monitoring and tuning of transaction processing. These tools can provide graphical interfaces for viewing system metrics, automated alerts for specific conditions, and detailed logs for post-event analysis. They can also suggest

tuning parameters based on observed performance data.

4. Performance Metrics: Important performance metrics for transaction processing include transaction throughput (the number of transactions processed per unit time), latency (the delay between a client request and the system response), and resource utilization (how efficiently the system's hardware and software resources are being used).

5. Importance of Monitoring and Tuning: Monitoring and tuning are critical for maintaining the performance, reliability, and efficiency of transaction processing systems. They can help identify and prevent potential problems before they affect system users, and they can ensure that the system is making the best possible use of its resources.

This section emphasizes the importance of proactive system management and the value of understanding the inner workings of the transaction processing lifecycle. By keeping a close eye on the system's performance and making adjustments as necessary, administrators can ensure that their mainframe transaction processing systems continue to perform optimally and meet their users' needs.

12.8 The Transaction Processing Lifecycle in the Modern Mainframe World

THE MAINFRAME TRANSACTION processing lifecycle has had to adapt and evolve to keep pace with the changes in the modern computing landscape. This section discusses these changes and how the lifecycle has adjusted to continue providing robust, reliable transaction processing. Here are the major topics covered:

1. Distributed Transactions: As businesses and technologies become increasingly interconnected, transactions often need to span multiple systems, databases, or even geographical locations. This creates unique challenges, such as coordinating and committing transactions across these different systems. The transaction processing lifecycle in a mainframe environment has evolved to handle these distributed transactions, using protocols like two-phase commit to ensure that all parts of the transaction either commit or abort together, maintaining data consistency.

2. Cloud Integration: With the rise of cloud computing, many organizations are adopting hybrid architectures that integrate mainframes with cloud-based systems. This creates new demands on the transaction processing lifecycle, including the need to communicate with cloud-based services and handle transactions that span both on-premise mainframes and cloud systems.

3. Scalability and Performance: The ever-increasing volume of data and transactions places more demand on mainframe systems. Modern transaction processing lifecycles must therefore prioritize scalability and performance, using techniques such as parallel processing, optimized resource utilization, and advanced queuing

mechanisms to handle high transaction loads effectively.

4. Security and Compliance: The modern mainframe world also brings new security and compliance requirements. Protecting sensitive data and adhering to regulations like GDPR or PCI-DSS is crucial. As such, security measures like encryption, secure protocols, and access control mechanisms are integral parts of the transaction processing lifecycle.

5. Modern Development Practices: Practices like Agile development, DevOps, and Continuous Integration/ Continuous Delivery (CI/CD) have changed how software is developed and deployed. The transaction processing lifecycle in modern mainframes has adapted to these changes, supporting more rapid and flexible deployment of new applications and updates.

By exploring these topics, this section illustrates how the transaction processing lifecycle has evolved to stay relevant and effective in the modern mainframe world. Despite the many changes in the technological landscape, the mainframe remains a cornerstone of enterprise computing, and its transaction processing capabilities continue to be vital for many businesses.

12.9 Conclusion

IN THE CONCLUSION OF Chapter 12, we highlight the significant themes that were discussed throughout the chapter and reflect on their importance in the context of mainframe environments.

Throughout this chapter, we have explored the transaction processing lifecycle in mainframe environments, beginning from the initial client request to the ultimate transaction completion and commitment. We have delved into the importance of every stage and the various factors that impact transaction processing, such as isolation, consistency, error handling, recovery mechanisms, and performance tuning.

The discussion also emphasized the role of different mainframe components and mechanisms during this lifecycle, including operating systems, databases, middleware, and programming languages. In addition, we covered the importance of monitoring the lifecycle to optimize transaction processing performance, and ensure data integrity and consistency.

The chapter also navigated the changing landscape of the transaction processing lifecycle in the modern era. The integration of distributed transactions, cloud computing, modern development practices, enhanced security measures, and increased compliance demands all play a pivotal role in the current and future trajectory of mainframe transaction processing.

Understanding the transaction processing lifecycle is vital for optimizing mainframe operations and adapting to modern computing trends. The lifecycle underscores the inherent strengths of mainframe systems in handling high-volume, high-throughput, and critical transaction processing tasks. As mainframes continue to evolve to meet the demands of modern enterprises, the principles and concepts of the transaction processing lifecycle remain as relevant as ever.

Chapter 13: Security in Mainframe Transaction Processing

——

Chapter 13, titled "Security in Mainframe Transaction Processing," covers the different aspects of security that are particularly relevant to the context of mainframe transaction processing. Here's a breakdown of the content within the chapter:

13.1 Introduction to Mainframe Transaction Processing Security: This section provides an overview of the importance of security in the context of mainframe transaction processing, highlighting the unique security considerations that come into play in such environments.

13.2 Security and Mainframe Hardware: This section explores how security is incorporated at the hardware level in mainframes, including hardware-based encryption, secure access features, and tamper-resistant designs.

13.3 Operating System Security: In this part, we examine the security measures built into mainframe operating systems, such as access controls, auditing capabilities, and security-related services and utilities.

13.4 Database Security: Here, we look at how security is enforced within mainframe databases, discussing features like data encryption, role-based access control, and security checks during transaction processing.

13.5 Middleware and Security: This section explains the role of middleware in security enforcement, covering topics like secure communication, data masking, and integration with other security mechanisms.

13.6 Programming Language Security: This part focuses on how various programming languages used in mainframe environments address security, with emphasis on language features that help prevent common security vulnerabilities.

13.7 Transaction Security: This section takes a detailed look at the security measures specific to transaction processing, such as secure transaction protocols, encryption of transaction data, and measures to prevent transaction fraud.

13.8 Security Monitoring and Compliance: Here, we cover the tools and techniques used for security monitoring in mainframe environments, and discuss the importance of compliance with various security standards and regulations.

13.9 Conclusion: The chapter concludes with a summary of the key points covered and a reflection on the importance of security in mainframe transaction processing.

13.1 Introduction to Mainframe Transaction Processing Security

THE "INTRODUCTION TO Mainframe Transaction Processing Security" sets the foundation for understanding the importance and implications of security in the world of mainframe transaction processing.

Security in mainframe transaction processing is of paramount importance because these systems often handle critical, sensitive, and confidential information. Banks, governments, and large corporations rely on mainframe systems to process high volumes of transactions accurately and securely.

The unique characteristics of mainframe transaction processing require tailored security considerations. For example, the high transaction volume, coupled with the need for simultaneous access by multiple users, necessitates robust mechanisms for access control and isolation.

This section also introduces some of the inherent security features of mainframes, such as hardware-based encryption and sophisticated access control systems. The focus on security in mainframe systems is underscored by their use in high-stakes applications such as financial transactions, where even minor vulnerabilities can have substantial implications.

In addition, this introduction covers the role of different layers in ensuring security - from the hardware and operating system to the database and middleware. Understanding these layers is crucial because security in such systems is not just about guarding against external threats but also about managing access, enforcing policies, and ensuring data integrity within the system.

By the end of this section, readers will appreciate the gravity of security considerations in mainframe transaction processing and the need for a multi-layered, comprehensive approach to protect these systems.

13.2 Security and Mainframe Hardware

THE "SECURITY AND MAINFRAME Hardware" section delves into how security measures are implemented right at the core of mainframe systems: the hardware. Mainframes are equipped with several security features at the hardware level that provide foundational security controls, which make them a preferred choice for processing sensitive and critical data.

One of the key security features at this level is hardware-based encryption. Encryption is the process of converting data into a format that cannot be understood without a decryption key. Hardware-based encryption mechanisms have dedicated processors to perform encryption and decryption tasks. This approach not only offloads the burden from the central processor (improving performance), but also provides a layer of security that is difficult to breach. In many mainframes, data is automatically encrypted when it is written to disk and decrypted when read, ensuring the protection of data at rest.

Secure access features are another essential aspect of mainframe hardware security. These include mechanisms for secure booting (ensuring the system boots only authorized and verified code), hardware firewalls (protecting the system at the network level), and intrusion detection systems (detecting unauthorized access attempts).

Lastly, many mainframes also have tamper-resistant or tamper-evident designs. These designs make it difficult to physically alter the hardware without detection. This could include sealed components, lockable casings, and alarms that trigger if someone attempts to open the case.

Through these features, mainframe systems provide a robust, built-in security layer at the hardware level, establishing a secure foundation on which the rest of the system operates.

13.3 Operating System Security

THE "OPERATING SYSTEM Security" section delves into the fundamental role that the operating system plays in maintaining a secure mainframe environment. Mainframe operating systems come with a suite of security features, services, and utilities to safeguard transactions and data.

Access control is a critical aspect of operating system security. It determines who can access the system, what they can do, and which resources they can use. This usually involves user authentication (verifying the identity of users) and authorization (determining what authenticated users are allowed to do). Mainframe operating systems often support advanced access control mechanisms, such as role-based access control (RBAC), which assigns permissions based on roles rather than individual users, and mandatory access control (MAC), which enforces access policies based on classification levels of information and users.

In addition to access control, mainframe operating systems also offer extensive auditing capabilities. Auditing is the process of recording and analyzing activities in a system to detect potential security breaches or policy violations. Operating systems typically log events like successful and failed login attempts, changes in user privileges, and modifications to critical system files. These logs can be analyzed manually or with automated tools to identify security incidents and trends.

Furthermore, mainframe operating systems come with a range of security-related services and utilities. These include encryption services for protecting data, intrusion detection systems for identifying unauthorized activities, and security management utilities for configuring security settings and policies.

Through these mechanisms, the operating system contributes to creating a robust security architecture for mainframe transaction processing, providing granular controls over user access, rigorous monitoring of system activities, and a toolkit for maintaining a secure system environment.

13.4 Database Security

THE "DATABASE SECURITY" section explores how mainframe databases implement security measures to protect sensitive data and ensure that transactions are executed securely.

One fundamental security feature in mainframe databases is data encryption. Data encryption transforms readable data into encoded data that can only be read or processed after it's been decrypted using a decryption key. This method protects data both at rest and in transit, preventing unauthorized access even if the data is intercepted or the storage is compromised. Many mainframe databases support a variety of encryption algorithms and provide facilities for secure key management.

Another key aspect of database security is access control, often implemented as role-based access control (RBAC). RBAC assigns permissions to roles, such as 'database admin' or 'data analyst', rather than individual users. Users are then assigned to these roles. RBAC is a flexible and scalable way to manage database access. It ensures that users have the minimum necessary permissions to perform their tasks, adhering to the principle of least privilege.

Security checks during transaction processing are also crucial in database security. Before executing a transaction, the database management system checks whether the user or application has the necessary permissions to perform the requested operations. This can include checking permissions for reading, writing, or modifying specific data. Some systems can also perform row-level or column-level security checks, providing even finer control over data access.

Security auditing is another feature provided by many database systems. This involves logging access and changes to data, as well as other security-relevant events. Audit logs can be used to detect suspicious activity, investigate incidents, or ensure compliance with security policies and regulations.

Through these measures, mainframe databases contribute significantly to the overall security of transaction processing. They provide robust defenses against unauthorized data access, data breaches, and other potential security threats.

13.5 Middleware and Security

THE "MIDDLEWARE AND Security" section delves into how middleware, as an intermediary layer of software that facilitates communication between different applications or systems, plays a crucial role in enforcing security.

One primary aspect of middleware security is ensuring secure communication. Middleware often provides support for secure communication protocols like SSL/TLS, enabling encrypted communication between different system components. This helps to ensure that data in transit cannot be intercepted or tampered with, protecting sensitive data as it is transmitted between applications, databases, or other systems.

Middleware can also play a significant role in data masking. Data masking is a process that obscures sensitive information in non-production environments. For instance, a middleware tool might replace personally identifiable information (PII) with fictional but realistic data when sending data from a production system to a development or testing system. This allows developers and testers to work with realistic data without exposing sensitive information.

Another important function of middleware is its integration with other security mechanisms. Middleware can interface with authentication and authorization systems, ensuring that only authenticated and authorized users or systems can access certain resources or perform certain actions. Middleware can also integrate with security monitoring tools, helping to detect and alert about suspicious activity or potential security threats.

Furthermore, middleware can play a role in implementing security policies and access control across disparate systems. By centralizing these functions in the middleware layer, organizations can enforce consistent security measures across different applications and systems, even if those systems use different technologies or are managed by different teams.

By taking on these responsibilities, middleware helps to ensure the security of mainframe transaction processing, protecting data integrity and confidentiality while facilitating secure, controlled access to resources.

13.6 Programming Language Security

THE "PROGRAMMING LANGUAGE Security" section of this chapter discusses the role that different programming languages play in maintaining security within mainframe environments. Here, we focus on how these languages have features and best practices to prevent common security vulnerabilities.

Programming languages commonly used in mainframe environments, like COBOL, PL/I, and even modern ones like Java and Python, have inherent security considerations.

1. COBOL: As an older language, it doesn't inherently include many modern security features. However, it's typically combined with mainframe security systems like RACF (Resource Access Control Facility), which control access to critical resources. This helps mitigate the potential security risks that could arise from its usage.

2. PL/I: Similar to COBOL, PL/I is often paired with mainframe security systems. However, it has more modern control structures which can help in writing more secure code.

3. Java: Being a modern language, Java has built-in security features, including its own security architecture, with features like bytecode verification, a security manager that defines customizable runtime access controls, and strong automatic memory management which can prevent common programming errors like buffer overflows that could lead to security vulnerabilities.

4. Python: Python encourages writing clean and readable code, which makes it easier to avoid security issues that come from complexity. It also comes with an extensive

standard library which includes several modules for implementing security protocols.

Regardless of the language used, following secure coding practices is crucial to avoid introducing security vulnerabilities. This can include techniques such as input validation (to prevent issues like SQL injection or cross-site scripting), avoiding unsafe functions or constructs known to lead to issues (like buffer overflows or race conditions), properly handling errors and exceptions to avoid leaking sensitive information, and so on.

In summary, while the programming languages used in mainframe transaction processing can vary greatly in terms of their built-in security features, the secure use of these languages is more dependent on how they are used – particularly the practices followed by developers in writing secure code and leveraging the security features and protections provided by the mainframe environment.

13.7 Transaction Security

THE "TRANSACTION SECURITY" section examines the key security measures employed during the process of transaction processing. These measures are critical to maintain the integrity, confidentiality, and availability of data while it's being processed.

1. Secure Transaction Protocols: Protocols like SSL/TLS are commonly used to secure the transmission of transaction data. These protocols provide end-to-end encryption of data in transit, protecting it from eavesdropping or tampering. In a mainframe environment, protocols like Enterprise Extensible Markup Language (EXML) might be used, which add additional security layers on top of standard HTTP.

2. Encryption of Transaction Data: Encryption is a fundamental aspect of transaction security. Sensitive data, such as credit card numbers or personally identifiable information (PII), is encrypted during transaction processing. This ensures that even if data is intercepted or accessed without authorization, it remains unintelligible and secure. In addition to data in transit, data at rest (stored data) is often encrypted too.

3. Measures to Prevent Transaction Fraud: Mainframes employ several mechanisms to prevent transaction fraud. These include robust authentication mechanisms (ensuring that only authorized individuals can initiate transactions), fine-grained access controls (ensuring individuals can only perform transactions within their allowed scope), and fraud detection systems (which use machine learning and other techniques to detect abnormal transaction patterns that might indicate fraud).

4. Audit Trails: Keeping detailed logs of transactions can assist in identifying and investigating potential security incidents. Audit trails keep track of who accessed what data, when, and what actions were taken. They're an essential tool for maintaining security, ensuring compliance, and providing visibility into transaction processing.

5. Transaction Integrity: Transaction processing systems in mainframes use mechanisms like two-phase commit to ensure that transactions are atomic, consistent, isolated, and durable (ACID). These properties are vital to prevent data corruption or loss in case of failures and ensure the reliability of transactions.

In summary, transaction security is a multi-faceted topic, involving not just the secure handling and transmission of data, but also measures to prevent fraud, ensure transaction integrity, and provide visibility and accountability through audit trails. It's a critical aspect of mainframe transaction processing security.

13.8 Security Monitoring and Compliance

"SECURITY MONITORING and Compliance" is a vital aspect of ensuring robust and ongoing security in mainframe transaction processing.

1. Security Monitoring: Security monitoring involves the continuous observation and analysis of system activity to detect potential security threats. This can involve the use of Security Information and Event Management (SIEM) tools that gather, normalize, and correlate log data from various sources to identify abnormal activities or patterns that might indicate a security incident. On mainframes, this includes monitoring access to sensitive data, changes to critical system files, failed login attempts, and so on. Additionally, anomaly detection techniques can be employed to identify behavior that deviates from established patterns, such as unusual transaction volumes or suspicious access patterns. In case of any potential threat, alerting mechanisms are triggered to inform security personnel for further investigation.

2. Compliance: Compliance refers to the adherence to various security standards and regulations. Depending on the industry and the type of data being processed, mainframe environments might need to comply with regulations such as the General Data Protection Regulation (GDPR) for data privacy, the Payment Card Industry Data Security Standard (PCI DSS) for payment information, or the Health Insurance Portability and Accountability Act (HIPAA) for health information. Compliance involves implementing the necessary security controls and regularly auditing these controls to ensure

their effectiveness. Non-compliance can lead to penalties, loss of customer trust, and other adverse consequences.

3. Regular Audits: Regular audits are performed to ensure that the system adheres to the established security policies and standards. These audits can be performed internally or by third-party organizations. Audits help identify any security gaps or vulnerabilities that need to be addressed and ensure that the system remains in compliance with all relevant regulations.

4. Incident Response: In case a security incident is detected, an incident response plan is triggered. This includes identifying the scope of the breach, containing it, eradicating the threat, and recovering from the incident. Post-incident, a thorough investigation is performed to learn from the incident and improve the security measures.

Overall, security monitoring and compliance are about staying vigilant, maintaining the adherence to the required security standards, and being prepared to respond effectively when security incidents occur. These measures provide an extra layer of protection to mainframe transaction processing environments, ensuring the confidentiality, integrity, and availability of data.

13.9 Conclusion

"CONCLUSION" IS THE final section of Chapter 13 that summarizes the key takeaways and underscores the significance of security in the context of mainframe transaction processing.

The security of mainframe transaction processing is a multifaceted and comprehensive aspect, involving different levels from hardware to software, from data storage to data transmission, and from system access to transaction execution.

1. Security and Mainframe Hardware: Security in mainframe transaction processing begins at the hardware level, where built-in encryption capabilities, secure access features, and tamper-resistant designs provide a foundational layer of protection.

2. Operating System and Database Security: The operating systems and databases that drive mainframe transaction processing also have essential roles to play in security. Through features such as robust access control mechanisms, auditing capabilities, data encryption, and security checks during transaction processing, they help ensure the confidentiality, integrity, and availability of data.

3. Middleware and Programming Language Security: Middleware and programming languages used in mainframes also contribute to security enforcement. Middleware helps in secure communication and data masking, while programming languages provide features to prevent common security vulnerabilities.

4. Transaction Security: Ensuring the security of transactions themselves is a critical aspect, encompassing secure

transaction protocols, encryption of transaction data, and measures to prevent transaction fraud.

5. Security Monitoring and Compliance: Monitoring security in real-time and maintaining compliance with security standards and regulations is key to identifying and responding to potential threats and ensuring ongoing security effectiveness.

The importance of security in mainframe transaction processing can't be overstated. As these systems often handle highly sensitive and valuable data, they are attractive targets for cybercriminals. Thus, understanding and implementing robust security measures is crucial. From ensuring compliance with data protection regulations to protecting against fraudulent transactions, the realm of mainframe transaction processing security is a vital area of study and practice.

As we move forward into an era of increasingly sophisticated cyber threats, the field of mainframe transaction processing security continues to evolve, underscoring the necessity for continuous learning, adaptation, and vigilance.

Part V: Advanced Concepts and Future Trends in Mainframe Transaction Processing

———

I n the final part of this book, we delve into advanced topics and explore the future trends of mainframe transaction processing. This part seeks to provide insights into complex concepts and methodologies that experts in the field employ, as well as to examine how the landscape of mainframe transaction processing is likely to evolve in the face of emerging technologies and changing business needs.

Chapter 14: Performance Tuning in Mainframe Transaction Processing

This chapter explores the art and science of performance tuning in the context of mainframe transaction processing. It covers techniques for monitoring performance, identifying bottlenecks, and implementing optimizations to ensure that mainframe transaction processing systems can handle high volumes of transactions efficiently and reliably.

Chapter 15: Advanced Transactional Models in Mainframes

In this chapter, we look beyond the traditional transaction processing models typically used in mainframes to examine more advanced and complex models. This includes distributed transactions, long-running transactions, and other sophisticated transactional models that offer increased flexibility and functionality in certain scenarios.

Chapter 16: Future Trends in Mainframe Transaction Processing

The final chapter of the book looks to the future, discussing emerging trends and technologies that are shaping the evolution of mainframe transaction processing. From the impact of cloud computing and artificial intelligence to the rise of real-time transaction processing, this chapter provides insights into where mainframe transaction processing is headed and how professionals in the field can prepare for these changes.

Chapter 14: Performance Tuning in Mainframe Transaction Processing

———

14.1 Introduction to Performance Tuning: This section introduces the concept of performance tuning in mainframe transaction processing. It highlights its importance, the factors that can affect performance, and the key objectives of tuning.

14.2 Monitoring Performance: Here, we discuss various techniques and tools for monitoring the performance of mainframe transaction processing systems. This includes tracking system utilization, response times, throughput, and other important performance indicators.

14.3 Identifying Performance Bottlenecks: This part covers methods for identifying and diagnosing performance bottlenecks. It looks at potential problem areas such as CPU usage, I/O operations, network latency, and software inefficiencies.

14.4 Optimization Techniques: This section dives into various optimization techniques that can be applied at different levels of the mainframe system, including hardware, operating system, middleware, databases, and application code.

14.5 Database Tuning: Here, we explore specific techniques for tuning databases in a mainframe environment. This involves strategies for data organization, query optimization, and efficient use of indexing and partitioning.

14.6 Tuning for Concurrency: This part focuses on strategies for optimizing mainframe systems to handle concurrent transactions effectively, discussing concepts like locking, deadlock prevention, and isolation levels.

14.7 Capacity Planning: This section looks at capacity planning as a proactive approach to performance tuning, explaining how to plan for growth and peak loads to ensure that mainframe systems can handle future demands.

14.8 Case Studies of Performance Tuning: This part presents some real-world case studies that illustrate the process of performance tuning in different scenarios.

14.9 Conclusion: The chapter wraps up with a summary of the key points discussed and a reflection on the role of performance tuning in ensuring the efficiency and reliability of mainframe transaction processing systems.

14.1 Introduction to Performance Tuning

PERFORMANCE TUNING in mainframe transaction processing is a critical activity that aims to optimize the system's performance and improve the efficiency of transaction processing tasks. The importance of performance tuning cannot be understated - it not only ensures optimal resource utilization but also significantly enhances system responsiveness, data throughput, and overall user experience.

Performance tuning in a mainframe context involves adjusting various parameters and system configurations, optimizing code, and managing resources more effectively to achieve better performance. It's a continuous process that involves monitoring, identifying bottlenecks, making necessary adjustments, and then repeating the process.

Several factors can affect the performance of mainframe transaction processing systems. These include hardware constraints (like processor speed, memory size, I/O capacity), operating system configurations, middleware settings, database structure and access mechanisms, network latency, and the efficiency of the application code itself.

The key objectives of performance tuning are manifold:

1. Improving Response Time: The time taken by the system to respond to a user request should be minimal. Performance tuning often aims to reduce this response time to provide a faster, more efficient user experience.
2. Increasing Throughput: This involves maximizing the number of transactions a system can handle in a given timeframe. The more transactions processed per unit of

time, the higher the system's throughput.

3. Optimal Resource Utilization: Resources such as CPU, memory, and storage are finite. Performance tuning aims to ensure these resources are used optimally and not wasted, thereby maximizing efficiency and cost-effectiveness.

4. Enhancing Scalability: As systems grow and demand increases, performance tuning can help ensure the system scales effectively to handle increased loads without a drop in performance.

In essence, performance tuning is about getting the most out of your mainframe transaction processing systems, making them more efficient, responsive, and capable of handling larger transaction loads.

14.2 Monitoring Performance

MONITORING PERFORMANCE is an essential part of performance tuning in mainframe transaction processing systems. It involves the continuous tracking and analyzing of various performance metrics to gain insights into the system's behavior, identify bottlenecks, and determine areas for improvement.

Key performance indicators include:

1. System Utilization: This involves monitoring the use of critical system resources, including CPU usage, memory consumption, I/O rates, and network bandwidth. High system utilization could indicate potential bottlenecks or areas where optimization might be needed.
2. Response Times: This metric measures the time it takes for a system to respond to a user request. By tracking response times, one can gauge the system's responsiveness and identify any slow-running operations that might need to be optimized.
3. Throughput: This refers to the number of transactions processed per unit of time. Monitoring throughput can provide insights into the system's capacity and efficiency.
4. Error Rates: This involves tracking system errors or failed transactions. A high error rate could indicate underlying problems that need to be addressed.

Several tools and techniques can be used for performance monitoring in mainframes:

- Performance Monitoring Software: Several software tools, like IBM's MainView or CA SYSVIEW, are designed specifically for mainframe performance monitoring. These tools can provide real-time statistics, alerts, and detailed reports on various system parameters.

- System Logs: Mainframe systems generate extensive logs that can be analyzed to track performance metrics and identify potential issues.
- Built-in OS Tools: Mainframe operating systems also often come with built-in utilities for performance monitoring. For example, IBM's z/OS includes Resource Measurement Facility (RMF) and Workload Manager (WLM) for tracking resource usage and managing workloads.
- Database Monitoring Tools: Tools like IBM's Db2 Monitor can be used to track the performance of mainframe databases, with metrics on query execution times, lock contention, and other important database performance indicators.

Performance monitoring is not a one-time activity but rather an ongoing process. Continuous monitoring allows for timely identification and resolution of performance issues, leading to more stable, efficient, and effective mainframe transaction processing.

14.3 Identifying Performance Bottlenecks

IDENTIFYING PERFORMANCE bottlenecks is a critical aspect of performance tuning in mainframe transaction processing systems. A bottleneck refers to a point in the system where the performance is limited or constrained, potentially leading to decreased throughput and increased response times.

1. CPU Usage: One common bottleneck can be high CPU usage. If the CPU is constantly running at high capacity, it could indicate inefficient code or a need for more processing power. Monitoring tools can help identify which processes or transactions are using the most CPU time.

2. I/O Operations: Another typical area for bottlenecks is I/O operations. Slow disk read/write operations or high disk utilization can significantly reduce performance. This could be due to inefficient database access, large data transfers, or hardware limitations.

3. Network Latency: In a distributed mainframe environment, network latency can become a significant performance bottleneck. Delays in data transmission can result in slow response times. Network monitoring tools can be used to identify such issues and optimize network configurations.

4. Software Inefficiencies: Software-related bottlenecks can stem from inefficient algorithms, sub-optimal database queries, excessive locking, or poorly configured middleware. Code profiling and database tuning can help uncover and resolve these bottlenecks.

The process of identifying bottlenecks often begins with a broad system overview, using monitoring tools to track system-wide performance metrics. Once potential problem areas are identified, more in-depth analysis can be performed to pinpoint the specific source of the bottleneck.

For example, if high CPU usage is detected, a developer might use a profiling tool to identify which part of the application code is causing the CPU strain. If the bottleneck is related to I/O operations, detailed I/O monitoring might reveal whether it's due to a hardware issue, inefficient database access patterns, or some other reason.

Identifying bottlenecks can be a complex and iterative process. However, by systematically narrowing down the areas of concern and using the right diagnostic tools, one can effectively identify the root cause and devise strategies to eliminate the bottleneck, thereby optimizing the system's performance.

14.4 Optimization Techniques

OPTIMIZATION TECHNIQUES in mainframe transaction processing involve implementing strategies that enhance the system's performance at various levels. This can include modifications to the hardware, operating system, middleware, databases, and application code. Let's discuss these in detail:

1. Hardware Optimization: Upgrading or properly configuring hardware components can significantly enhance performance. This might involve adding more memory, improving disk storage, or upgrading processors. Another aspect can be network optimization, like adjusting network configurations to reduce latency.

2. Operating System Optimization: Adjusting the settings of the operating system can help ensure resources are utilized effectively. This can include optimizing process scheduling, adjusting memory management policies, or tweaking I/O subsystems. For instance, in IBM's z/OS, Workload Manager (WLM) can be used to manage system resources effectively.

3. Middleware Optimization: Middleware acts as a bridge between different applications, databases, and other system components. Optimizing middleware can involve configuring it for optimal data transmission, reducing message queue bottlenecks, and ensuring efficient connection pooling.

4. Database Optimization: This often involves query optimization, indexing, partitioning, and efficient transaction management. Database administrators can use tools like DB2's Query Monitor and Index Advisor to help in identifying inefficient queries or determining optimal

indexing strategies.

5. Application Code Optimization: This might involve rewriting inefficient code, optimizing algorithms, or avoiding expensive operations. For instance, reducing the complexity of an algorithm or minimizing the frequency of disk I/O operations can improve performance significantly. Code profiling tools can help identify code sections that are CPU-intensive or that result in blocking or deadlocks.

6. Parallel Processing: Utilizing parallel processing can help take full advantage of the mainframe's multi-core architecture. Tasks that can be performed concurrently should be designed to run in parallel to speed up processing time.

Optimization is an ongoing process, and it's important to monitor system performance continually. This helps to identify new bottlenecks as they emerge and to assess the effectiveness of the optimizations implemented. It's also important to consider the trade-offs associated with each optimization technique. For instance, while adding more memory can improve performance, it also increases costs, so the benefits need to be weighed against the costs.

14.5 Database Tuning

DATABASE TUNING IN a mainframe environment involves a set of strategies that improve database performance and ensure efficient use of resources. This includes considerations for how data is organized, the optimization of queries, and the efficient use of indexing and partitioning. Let's delve into these aspects:

1. Data Organization: How data is stored and organized in a database can have a significant impact on performance. This can include considering the physical design of the database, such as how tables are structured and how fields are defined. For example, you might choose to normalize data to minimize redundancy, or denormalize it to reduce the number of joins required in queries.

2. Query Optimization: Optimizing the SQL queries that are used to access and manipulate data is another critical aspect of database tuning. This can involve rewriting queries to make them more efficient, reducing the amount of data that needs to be scanned. Database systems typically have a query optimizer that helps in this regard, but understanding its workings can allow you to write more efficient queries.

3. Indexing: The use of indexes can significantly speed up data retrieval. However, creating and maintaining indexes also requires resources, so you need to strike a balance. The key is to create indexes on columns that are frequently used in WHERE clauses, JOIN conditions, and ORDER BY clauses. But excessive indexing can lead to slower insert and update operations.

4. Partitioning: Partitioning is a technique where a database or a table is split into smaller, more manageable parts,

which can be stored across different physical locations. This can improve performance by allowing queries to scan smaller amounts of data. Partitioning can be done in various ways, such as range partitioning (based on a range of values), list partitioning (based on a list of values), or hash partitioning (based on a hash function).

5. Concurrency Control: Efficient handling of simultaneous transactions can help in reducing waiting time and deadlocks. This can involve choosing appropriate isolation levels based on the requirements of each transaction.

6. Buffer Pool Tuning: Buffer pools keep frequently accessed data in memory to reduce disk I/O operations. Adjusting the size of these pools and determining which data to keep in them can significantly affect performance.

7. Database Maintenance: Regular database maintenance tasks, such as updating statistics, rebuilding indexes, and defragmenting data can help keep performance optimal.

Database tuning is a complex, ongoing task that requires a deep understanding of the database system's inner workings. It is also essential to monitor database performance continuously and adjust strategies as needed to adapt to changing workloads and requirements.

14.6 Tuning for Concurrency

IN A MAINFRAME TRANSACTION processing environment, concurrency is the ability to handle multiple transactions at the same time. Effective concurrency can significantly improve system throughput and overall performance. However, it comes with challenges such as ensuring data consistency and avoiding conflicts. Let's explore some strategies for tuning mainframe systems for effective concurrency:

1. Locking: Locking is a fundamental concept in concurrent transaction processing. It prevents multiple transactions from modifying the same data simultaneously, ensuring data consistency. However, the use of locks should be optimized to minimize the contention for resources. For instance, using row-level locking instead of table-level locking can improve concurrency by allowing transactions to work with different rows simultaneously.

2. Deadlock Prevention: Deadlocks occur when two or more transactions are waiting for each other to release resources. Deadlocks can severely impact performance as they cause transactions to wait indefinitely. Strategies to prevent deadlocks include using a consistent order for acquiring locks, using timeout periods for locks, and using deadlock detection algorithms that can identify and resolve deadlocks when they occur.

3. Isolation Levels: The level of isolation determines how much a transaction is isolated from other concurrent transactions. Higher isolation levels offer more consistency but can reduce concurrency and performance. Lower isolation levels improve performance and concurrency but may lead to issues like dirty reads, non-repeatable reads, or

phantom reads. Therefore, choosing the right isolation level based on application requirements is crucial for optimizing concurrency.

4. Optimistic and Pessimistic Concurrency Control: Pessimistic concurrency control assumes that conflicts will occur and uses locks to prevent them. This is suitable for environments where contention is high. On the other hand, optimistic concurrency control assumes conflicts are rare and allows transactions to proceed without locks, checking for conflicts only at the commit time. This is ideal for read-heavy workloads with less contention.

5. Lock Escalation: Some systems use lock escalation, where many lower-level locks (like row or page locks) are converted into higher-level locks (like table locks) when a certain threshold is reached. While this can save system resources, it can also reduce concurrency. Therefore, managing the threshold for lock escalation can help balance resource usage and concurrency.

6. Use of Transaction Logs: Transaction logs record all changes made during a transaction. In case of conflicts, they can help roll back a transaction to its previous state, mitigating the impact on the system.

Remember, tuning for concurrency is a balancing act. The goal is to achieve a high level of concurrency while ensuring data integrity and consistency. Regular monitoring and adjustment are essential to maintain optimal performance.

14.7 Capacity Planning

IN THE CONTEXT OF MAINFRAME transaction processing, capacity planning is a strategic activity that ensures the system can meet future transaction loads. It involves understanding the current system's capabilities, forecasting future demands, and making necessary adjustments to hardware, software, and system configurations. The objective is to maintain optimal performance, avoid system overloads, and manage costs effectively.

1. Understanding the Current System: The first step in capacity planning is to understand the current system's capabilities. This involves monitoring and documenting the performance of the system under different load conditions. Key performance indicators like CPU utilization, memory usage, I/O operations, network bandwidth usage, transaction response times, and system throughput need to be tracked and analyzed.

2. Forecasting Future Demand: Once a baseline of the system's current performance is established, the next step is to forecast future transaction loads. This involves understanding the business's growth plans, expected increases in users or transactions, and potential peaks in system usage due to events like sales or promotions. Analytical methods or modeling techniques can be used to predict the impact of these factors on system performance.

3. Scenario Analysis and Testing: Different scenarios based on the projected growth and peak load conditions are created and tested to understand how the system would behave. Stress testing and load testing can be performed to identify potential bottlenecks and performance issues.

4. Making Necessary Adjustments: Based on the results of the

testing, necessary adjustments can be made to the system. This might involve upgrading hardware (like adding more memory or CPU), optimizing software configurations, improving database design, or changing network configurations.

5. Plan for Scalability: Planning for scalability involves designing the system so that capacity can be easily added when needed. This could involve strategies like cloud-based resources for elasticity, modular system design, or use of load balancing techniques.

6. Regular Reviews: Capacity planning is not a one-time activity. Regular reviews and updates to the capacity plan are necessary as business needs, system loads, and technology evolve.

Effective capacity planning can prevent system slowdowns or crashes, ensure smooth performance during peak loads, and avoid unnecessary expenditure on resources that are not needed. It aligns IT capabilities with business needs and paves the way for sustainable growth.

14.8 Case Studies of Performance Tuning

CASE STUDIES ARE AN effective way to understand the practical application of performance tuning. They allow us to learn from real-world scenarios and understand the challenges faced and strategies used in optimizing mainframe transaction processing systems. Here are summaries of a couple of such cases:

1. Case Study 1 - Financial Institution Database Tuning: A large financial institution noticed a gradual increase in response times for their transaction processing system, which was adversely impacting their customer service. On investigation, they found that the database access was a major bottleneck. The indexes on their large databases were not optimally designed, leading to slow data retrieval. By analyzing the most frequent queries and modifying the database indexes, they were able to drastically reduce query times and improve overall system performance.

2. Case Study 2 - Retailer's Holiday Sales Peak Load Management: A major online retailer was preparing for the holiday season sales, a period known for peak transaction loads. They conducted a detailed capacity planning exercise. They projected the expected increase in transactions, performed stress tests, and identified that the existing system would not be able to handle the expected load. To address this, they scaled up their mainframe resources, optimized their application code, and implemented a load-balancing solution. As a result, they were able to handle the holiday sales peak without any system slowdowns or crashes.

3. Case Study 3 - Telecommunication Provider's Concurrency Tuning: A global telecommunications

provider was experiencing issues with their transaction processing system during peak hours. On close inspection, they realized that the handling of concurrent transactions was causing system contention and deadlocks. By adjusting the isolation levels and implementing advanced locking mechanisms, they improved the system's capability to handle concurrent transactions, reducing deadlocks and enhancing overall system performance.

Each of these cases illustrates the principles and techniques of performance tuning in action. They underscore the importance of understanding the system's behavior, identifying bottlenecks, and implementing targeted optimizations to enhance performance.

14.9 Conclusion

PERFORMANCE TUNING is a critical aspect of maintaining the efficiency and reliability of mainframe transaction processing systems. It involves various facets, such as system monitoring, identification of performance bottlenecks, optimization at multiple levels, database tuning, and handling concurrency.

Monitoring performance enables organizations to keep track of key metrics like system utilization, response times, and throughput. This proactive approach helps identify potential issues before they escalate and impact system performance. It includes employing specialized tools to capture relevant metrics and gain insights into system performance.

Identifying performance bottlenecks is the next significant aspect. Bottlenecks can occur at several points in the system, such as CPU usage, I/O operations, network latency, or even within software. Efficient identification and resolution of these bottlenecks can significantly improve system performance.

Performance tuning also involves optimization at the hardware, operating system, middleware, databases, and application code levels. Each level has its unique set of considerations and techniques, which, when applied correctly, can contribute to improved performance.

Database tuning and concurrency management are two specialized areas within performance tuning. They involve strategies for data organization, query optimization, efficient use of indexing and partitioning, handling concurrent transactions, and implementing correct isolation levels.

Capacity planning is a crucial proactive strategy for performance tuning. It involves planning for growth and peak loads, ensuring the system is adequately equipped to handle future demands.

Through real-world case studies, we also saw how these strategies and techniques are applied in practice, providing tangible improvements in system performance.

In conclusion, performance tuning plays a pivotal role in ensuring that mainframe transaction processing systems operate at peak efficiency. By applying the techniques discussed in this chapter, organizations can significantly enhance their system performance, ultimately leading to improved service delivery and customer satisfaction.

Chapter 15: Advanced Transactional Models in Mainframes

15.1 Introduction to Advanced Transactional Models: This section provides an overview of the advanced transactional models used in mainframes, discussing their significance and the benefits they offer over basic transactional models.

15.2 Two-Phase Commit Protocol: An in-depth examination of the two-phase commit protocol, an advanced transactional model that ensures distributed transactions maintain consistency across all participating databases.

15.3 Three-Phase Commit Protocol: This part discusses the three-phase commit protocol, a further advancement over the two-phase commit that adds an additional layer of security to prevent blocking in case of failures.

15.4 Long-Lived Transactions: Here we look at the concept of long-lived transactions, exploring how they are managed and maintained in mainframe environments.

15.5 Nested Transactions: This section examines nested transactions, a model that allows transactions to be embedded within other transactions for improved organization and error recovery.

15.6 Parallel Transactions: A discussion on parallel transactions, explaining how they can be used to improve the efficiency and performance of transaction processing systems.

15.7 Saga Transactions: An exploration of saga transactions, a model designed for handling long-lived transactions by breaking them down into a series of smaller, isolated transactions.

15.8 Transaction Models in the Modern Mainframe World: This part discusses how advanced transactional models fit into the modern mainframe landscape, explaining how they have evolved to cater to the needs of distributed, cloud-based, and microservice architectures.

15.9 Conclusion: The chapter concludes with a summary of the key points discussed, reflecting on the importance of understanding advanced transactional models in a mainframe environment.

15.1 Introduction to Advanced Transactional Models

ADVANCED TRANSACTIONAL models are crucial for maintaining the integrity, reliability, and efficiency of transaction processing in modern mainframe environments. While basic transactional models provide the foundation for executing and managing transactions, advanced models offer more sophisticated techniques that cater to the complexities of modern IT infrastructures.

These advanced transactional models include concepts like distributed transactions, long-lived transactions, nested transactions, parallel transactions, and saga transactions, among others. They are particularly important in environments where transactions span across multiple systems or databases, have to be performed over an extended period, or involve multiple parallel operations.

One of the main benefits of advanced transactional models is their ability to ensure data consistency and system reliability even in the face of failure conditions. They employ mechanisms such as two-phase or three-phase commit protocols to ensure that a transaction is either fully committed on all involved systems or fully rolled back, preventing situations where a transaction is partially completed, which could lead to data inconsistency.

Another significant advantage is their ability to improve system efficiency. Models like parallel transactions and nested transactions allow for greater concurrency and better organization of transactional operations, leading to improved system throughput and response times.

Finally, advanced transactional models are also designed to provide better error recovery and isolation mechanisms. This is particularly important for long-lived and saga transactions, where the ability to handle errors in individual operations without affecting the entire transaction can be crucial.

Overall, understanding these advanced transactional models is key to effectively managing and optimizing mainframe transaction processing systems in the face of modern computing challenges. They represent the evolution of transaction management to accommodate increasingly complex, distributed, and demanding business processes.

15.2 Two-Phase Commit Protocol

THE TWO-PHASE COMMIT (2PC) protocol is a standard in distributed transaction processing and is a cornerstone of ensuring data consistency across multiple database systems involved in a transaction. This protocol provides an "all-or-nothing" approach, ensuring that a transaction either fully commits on all systems or is entirely rolled back if any single system fails during the transaction process.

The protocol works as the name suggests - in two phases:

1. Prepare Phase (Voting Phase): In this phase, the coordinator (a designated system or process managing the transaction) sends a prepare message to all the participants (the systems or processes involved in the transaction) asking if they can commit the transaction. Each participant executes the transaction up to the point of commitment but doesn't actually commit it yet. They then respond to the coordinator with a vote. If the transaction was executed successfully, they vote 'yes,' indicating they are ready to commit. If there were any issues, they vote 'no,' signaling they cannot commit.

2. Commit Phase (Completion Phase): The second phase depends on the votes received from the participants. If all participants vote 'yes,' the coordinator sends a 'commit' message to all participants. Each participant then fully commits the transaction and sends an acknowledgement back to the coordinator. If any participant votes 'no' or a timeout occurs and the coordinator doesn't receive all the votes, the coordinator sends a 'rollback' message to all participants. Each participant then undoes the transaction, ensuring data consistency.

The two-phase commit protocol is a block-structured protocol, meaning that once a coordinator has sent out the prepare request, it must wait for replies from all participants before proceeding. This characteristic makes the protocol resilient to failures but can also lead to situations where resources are held for longer than necessary, potentially impacting system performance.

Understanding and properly implementing the two-phase commit protocol is essential for any system architect or developer working with distributed transactions in a mainframe or any distributed environment. While the protocol ensures data consistency, its limitations must also be considered, and additional strategies may need to be used to prevent potential performance issues.

15.3 Three-Phase Commit Protocol

THE THREE-PHASE COMMIT (3PC) protocol is an enhancement over the Two-Phase Commit (2PC) protocol designed to address a specific problem with 2PC: in the event of a network partition or coordinator failure during the commit phase, participants may be left in a state of uncertainty, not knowing whether to commit or abort the transaction. This could lead to a "blocking" situation where resources remain locked until the coordinator can recover.

The 3PC protocol introduces an additional phase to overcome this problem. The protocol still maintains the atomicity of transactions across distributed systems, ensuring that a transaction either fully commits on all systems or is fully aborted. However, it adds another phase that allows participants to unblock themselves without the need for the coordinator's recovery.

The three phases are as follows:

1. CanCommit?: This is similar to the voting phase in 2PC. The coordinator sends a 'CanCommit?' message to all participants asking if they can commit the transaction. Each participant executes the transaction up to the point of commitment but does not commit yet. They then respond with either 'Yes' or 'No'.

2. PreCommit / Abort: If all participants responded with 'Yes', the coordinator sends a 'PreCommit' message, or else it sends an 'Abort' message. When participants receive the 'PreCommit' message, they enter the 'Prepared' state where they are ready to commit but wait for a 'doCommit' message from the coordinator. If they receive 'Abort', they undo the transaction and send an 'Ack' message to the coordinator.

3. DoCommit / Abort: If the coordinator receives 'Ack' from all participants, it sends the 'doCommit' message, prompting the participants to finally commit the transaction and send an 'Ack' back. If the coordinator doesn't receive an 'Ack' from all participants within a given timeframe, it sends an 'Abort' message.

This added phase in 3PC allows for non-blocking behavior, which can be a significant advantage in certain circumstances. However, it also adds extra complexity and overhead to the transaction processing, so it needs to be used judiciously and only when necessary.

15.4 Long-Lived Transactions

LONG-LIVED TRANSACTIONS, as their name suggests, are transactions that exist over a long duration, sometimes even for weeks or months. They differ from traditional short-lived transactions, which typically last only a few milliseconds or seconds and maintain the ACID properties (Atomicity, Consistency, Isolation, Durability) throughout their lifecycle.

Long-lived transactions pose certain unique challenges, primarily due to their longevity. For instance, locking resources for a long period can lead to system bottlenecks, hence traditional locking mechanisms are not suitable. Similarly, maintaining isolation over a prolonged period may not be feasible or desirable. Therefore, alternative strategies and mechanisms are required to manage long-lived transactions effectively.

A common approach is to break down the long-lived transaction into a series of short-lived subtransactions, each of which can maintain ACID properties independently. This approach provides better system performance and reduces the chance of long-term resource locking. However, managing and coordinating these subtransactions can be complex.

Compensating transactions can also be used to handle the longevity of such transactions. A compensating transaction is a transaction that undoes the work of a previous transaction. For instance, if a long-lived transaction needs to be rolled back after a certain point, instead of undoing all the operations, a compensating transaction can be executed to reverse the effect of the initial transaction.

Mainframe systems, with their powerful processing capabilities and sophisticated transaction management facilities, are well equipped to handle long-lived transactions. They offer robust support for both subtransactions and compensating transactions, along with advanced concurrency control mechanisms that optimize resource usage and prevent conflicts.

Overall, the management of long-lived transactions is an important aspect of advanced transactional models in mainframes, and it requires a deep understanding of transaction concepts, system characteristics, and application requirements.

15.5 Nested Transactions

NESTED TRANSACTIONS are a type of advanced transaction model in which a transaction can contain other transactions within it. These 'subtransactions' or 'child transactions' are initiated and completed within the scope of the 'parent' or 'outer' transaction. The key benefit of this model is that it provides more granular control over transaction execution and enhances error recovery capabilities.

The structure of nested transactions forms a hierarchy or tree-like structure. If an error occurs in one of the subtransactions, that subtransaction can be individually rolled back without impacting the entire outer transaction. This approach allows for more refined error handling and can reduce the amount of work that needs to be redone in the event of a failure.

Let's consider an example. Suppose an outer transaction involves updating customer records in a mainframe database, and there are several steps involved like updating the customer's contact details, their order history, and their payment information. Each of these steps could be managed as separate subtransactions within the overall transaction. If an error occurs while updating the payment information, only that subtransaction needs to be rolled back and retried, while the other updates remain intact.

Nested transactions also have implications for resource locking and concurrency control. Subtransactions can acquire and release locks independently of the parent transaction, which can help improve concurrency and system throughput. However, managing nested transactions also adds complexity to the transaction management process.

Overall, nested transactions are a powerful tool in the arsenal of mainframe transaction processing. They offer greater flexibility and improved error recovery, but they also require careful handling to ensure data consistency and system stability.

15.6 Parallel Transactions

PARALLEL TRANSACTIONS are a type of advanced transaction model that allows multiple transactions to be executed concurrently. This is often used to improve the efficiency and performance of transaction processing systems by leveraging the power of modern multi-core processors and high-speed networks.

In a mainframe environment, managing parallel transactions involves several key aspects:

1. Concurrency Control: This involves managing access to shared resources to prevent conflicts and ensure data consistency. Techniques such as locking, optimistic concurrency control, and multi-version concurrency control can be used to manage concurrent access.
2. Transaction Scheduling: This involves determining the order in which concurrent transactions are executed. The goal is to optimize the use of system resources and minimize the chance of conflicts.
3. Load Balancing: In distributed systems, load balancing strategies can be used to distribute transactions across different nodes, optimizing resource usage and ensuring a high level of system performance.
4. Recovery Mechanisms: With parallel transactions, it is important to have robust mechanisms in place for recovering from failures. This might involve keeping track of the state of each transaction so that the system can roll back or restart transactions as necessary.

Parallel transactions can greatly enhance the throughput and responsiveness of a mainframe transaction processing system, particularly in situations where there is a high volume of transactions. However, they also add complexity to the system and require sophisticated management techniques to ensure data consistency and system stability.

The implementation of parallel transactions is guided by the principles of ACID (Atomicity, Consistency, Isolation, Durability), ensuring that even when transactions are processed in parallel, the system maintains data integrity and consistency.

15.7 Saga Transactions

SAGA TRANSACTIONS ARE a type of advanced transaction model that is particularly suitable for long-lived transactions and distributed systems. A saga is a sequence of local transactions where each transaction update is followed by a defined compensating transaction that would undo the update if it was successfully completed. The compensating transactions provide a means to maintain consistency when a failure happens during the execution of a saga.

Saga transactions are broken down into multiple, smaller, and isolated transactions, each of which can be undone by its corresponding compensating transaction. This approach has several advantages:

1. Resilience: Because each transaction in a saga is isolated, a failure in one transaction does not necessarily cause the entire saga to fail. The system can simply execute the compensating transactions to rollback changes and maintain consistency.
2. Efficiency: Saga transactions can increase the overall efficiency of a system by enabling concurrent execution of non-conflicting transactions.
3. Availability: Since saga transactions do not hold long-term locks, they allow for high availability in distributed systems where network partitions can cause traditional locking schemes to become untenable.

However, there are also challenges associated with saga transactions. The management of compensating transactions can be complex, particularly in the event of failures. There are also semantic issues that arise from partial execution of sagas, as the system has to ensure a logical consistency when compensating transactions are executed.

In the context of mainframes, saga transactions are an important tool for managing complex, distributed transactions across multiple resources. This advanced transactional model provides a way to maintain consistency and reliability while also supporting the scalability and flexibility of modern mainframe environments.

15.8 Transaction Models in the Modern Mainframe World

AS MAINFRAME SYSTEMS continue to evolve to adapt to the modern digital landscape, advanced transaction models have become increasingly important to handle the complexities of modern applications and services. This section examines how these models have been adopted and adapted to fit into modern mainframe environments, particularly in relation to distributed, cloud-based, and microservice architectures.

1. Distributed Systems: With distributed systems, transactions are no longer confined to a single system; they span across different systems and networks. This has led to the adoption of protocols like two-phase commit and three-phase commit, designed to ensure consistency across distributed systems. Nested transactions and saga transactions also become particularly useful in managing complex, distributed transactions.

2. Cloud-based Architectures: With the shift to the cloud, transactional models have to account for aspects such as elasticity, on-demand scaling, and geo-distribution. As such, long-lived transactions, saga transactions, and parallel transactions are employed to maintain high levels of availability and consistency, despite potential network latency or failures.

3. Microservices Architectures: Microservices introduce a whole new level of distribution, where each service may have its own database. As such, coordinating transactions across these services can be challenging. Saga transactions have become particularly significant in this context, as they allow a large transaction to be broken down into smaller,

manageable pieces that each microservice can handle independently.

In all these contexts, it's important to strike a balance between maintaining data consistency and ensuring high performance. Thus, the choice of transaction model will depend on the specific requirements of the system and the nature of the transactions it handles. Advanced transactional models offer more flexibility and control, making them essential tools in the modern mainframe world.

15.9 Conclusion

THIS CHAPTER'S CONCLUSION underlines the significance of grasping advanced transactional models in the context of a mainframe environment. As mainframe systems continue to evolve, advanced transactional models have become more prominent due to their ability to handle complex and distributed transactions effectively, maintaining data consistency and transaction integrity across multiple systems and services.

Key points discussed in the chapter include:

1. Two-Phase Commit Protocol: This model ensures that distributed transactions maintain consistency across all participating databases. It uses a coordinator to ensure that all parts of a transaction are either committed or aborted, preserving atomicity and consistency.
2. Three-Phase Commit Protocol: A more robust model than the two-phase commit protocol, it introduces an additional 'pre-commit' phase to avoid blocking in the case of coordinator failure.
3. Long-Lived Transactions: Long-lived transactions are critical for operations that cannot be completed immediately and need to maintain their state over an extended period.
4. Nested Transactions: These allow transactions to be embedded within other transactions, improving organization, error recovery, and the ability to handle complex operations.
5. Parallel Transactions: By allowing transactions to be processed simultaneously, parallel transactions can significantly enhance the efficiency and performance of

transaction processing systems.

6. Saga Transactions: Saga transactions break down long-lived transactions into a series of smaller, isolated transactions, improving manageability and error recovery.

7. Adapting to the Modern Mainframe World: The evolution of mainframes to accommodate distributed, cloud-based, and microservice architectures has necessitated the adaptation of these advanced transactional models.

Understanding these models is vital for managing transactions effectively in complex and evolving mainframe environments. As the technology landscape continues to change, mainframes, with their reliability, robustness, and advanced transactional capabilities, remain at the heart of many critical business processes.

Chapter 16: Future Trends in Mainframe Transaction Processing

This chapter provides an overview of the future trends and predictions for mainframe transaction processing. It will look at the emerging technologies, methods, and strategies that are likely to shape the evolution of mainframes in the coming years.

Outline:

16.1 Introduction to Future Trends: This section provides an overview of the changing landscape of mainframe transaction processing, discussing the importance of anticipating future trends.

16.2 Cloud Integration: This part looks at how mainframes are increasingly integrating with cloud-based technologies, and what this means for transaction processing.

16.3 Big Data and Analytics: Here, we examine how the rise of big data and advanced analytics techniques are impacting transaction processing on mainframes.

16.4 Machine Learning and AI: This section explores the potential application of machine learning and artificial intelligence in mainframe environments, particularly in transaction processing.

16.5 Security Advances: This part looks at upcoming security technologies and methodologies that are likely to influence the way mainframe systems are protected.

16.6 Quantum Computing and Mainframes: A discussion on the potential impact of quantum computing on mainframe transaction processing.

16.7 Sustainability and Green Computing: This section looks at the trend towards more energy-efficient mainframe technologies, and the implications for transaction processing.

16.8 Conclusion: The chapter concludes with a summary of the key future trends discussed and a reflection on the evolving nature of mainframe transaction processing.

16.1 Introduction to Future Trends

AS WITH ANY TECHNOLOGY, mainframe transaction processing isn't static. It continues to evolve in response to changing business needs, technological advances, and industry trends. Staying abreast of these trends allows businesses to better leverage their mainframe systems and ensure they continue to deliver value.

Future trends in mainframe transaction processing may be influenced by factors such as advancements in hardware and software technologies, the increasing need for integration with other systems (including cloud-based services), and emerging practices in data management and security. It's also important to consider trends from a wider technological landscape perspective, such as the rise of machine learning, artificial intelligence, quantum computing, and green computing initiatives.

Understanding these trends is crucial for anyone involved in managing, developing, or making decisions about mainframe systems. It allows for more informed planning and decision-making, ensuring that mainframe systems continue to meet the needs of the organization effectively and efficiently.

Overall, the changing landscape of mainframe transaction processing poses both challenges and opportunities. While new technologies and methodologies can require investment and adjustments, they also offer the potential for improved performance, greater efficiency, enhanced security, and other benefits. By staying ahead of these trends, businesses can ensure they are well-positioned to leverage these opportunities.

16.2 Cloud Integration

CLOUD INTEGRATION HAS become a significant trend in the mainframe transaction processing world, prompted by the vast array of benefits offered by cloud computing. Cloud technologies offer scalability, flexibility, and cost-effectiveness, which are highly appealing characteristics for businesses in today's rapidly changing environment.

When it comes to transaction processing, the integration of mainframes with the cloud has several key implications:

1. Hybrid Transaction Processing: Many organizations are exploring hybrid transaction processing models where part of the workload is managed by the mainframe and part is managed in the cloud. This can offer greater scalability and flexibility, as additional cloud resources can be quickly brought online as needed.

2. Cloud-based Databases: With the rise of cloud-based databases, mainframes are increasingly interacting with these databases for transaction processing. This interaction requires efficient and secure networking protocols, data translation capabilities, and often sophisticated synchronization to maintain consistency.

3. Mainframe as a Service (MaaS): With cloud technologies, there's a trend towards providing "Mainframe as a Service". Here, mainframe capabilities are offered via the cloud, allowing organizations to leverage mainframe transaction processing capabilities without the need for significant on-premise hardware.

4. Application Modernization: As organizations move more services to the cloud, they often take the opportunity to

modernize their mainframe applications. This can involve refactoring legacy COBOL applications to more modern languages that are better supported in cloud environments, such as Java or Python.

5. Disaster Recovery and Continuity: Cloud technologies can significantly improve an organization's disaster recovery capabilities. By replicating data and applications in the cloud, businesses can quickly recover from a mainframe outage, ensuring continuity of transaction processing capabilities.

It's essential to consider security and compliance when integrating mainframes with cloud technologies, as sensitive transaction data will often be transferred between on-premise mainframes and cloud-based services. As such, robust encryption, secure protocols, and careful management of access rights are all crucial.

16.3 Big Data and Analytics

THE ADVENT OF BIG DATA and advanced analytics has significantly impacted the world of mainframe transaction processing. With the massive amounts of data generated by transactions, mainframes have evolved to become critical components in an organization's data analytics strategy. Here's how these trends are reshaping the landscape:

1. Data Mining and Business Intelligence: Transaction data stored in mainframes is a rich source of information for business intelligence. By applying data mining techniques to this data, organizations can gain insights into customer behavior, transaction patterns, and operational efficiency. This allows them to make informed business decisions, enhance customer service, and streamline processes.

2. Real-time Analytics: Mainframes are increasingly being equipped with tools to perform real-time analytics. By analyzing transaction data in real time, organizations can immediately detect fraud, identify opportunities, or respond to market changes. For example, credit card companies can use real-time analytics to detect unusual transaction patterns that might indicate fraudulent activity.

3. Machine Learning: Machine learning techniques can be used to analyze transaction data and predict future trends or behaviors. For example, machine learning algorithms can be used to predict transaction volumes based on historical data, enabling organizations to better manage capacity and maintain performance.

4. Data Virtualization: Data virtualization technologies allow disparate data sources, including mainframes, to be treated

as a single, virtual database. This simplifies data management and enhances the ability to perform complex analytics across multiple data sources.

5. Integration with Big Data Platforms: To enable advanced analytics, mainframes are increasingly integrated with big data platforms like Hadoop or Spark. This allows large volumes of transaction data to be efficiently processed and analyzed using the computational power of these platforms.

6. Data Privacy and Security: With the increasing use of transaction data for analytics, maintaining data privacy and security has become even more critical. Mainframes are renowned for their robust security features, making them well-equipped for managing sensitive transaction data in compliance with regulations like GDPR or CCPA.

As with other future trends, integrating big data and analytics into mainframe transaction processing needs to be done thoughtfully, balancing the need for insights and real-time decision making with the need to protect data and maintain system performance.

16.4 Machine Learning and AI

MACHINE LEARNING (ML) and Artificial Intelligence (AI) technologies are becoming increasingly integral in the modern world of IT, and mainframe transaction processing is no exception. The potential applications of these technologies in mainframes span several areas, particularly in improving efficiency, predicting system performance, enhancing security, and driving business decisions.

1. Predictive Analytics: ML can analyze patterns in historical transaction data to predict future behaviors. For example, machine learning algorithms could forecast periods of high transaction load, allowing for preemptive system scaling. Additionally, these predictions can help in capacity planning and identifying potential performance bottlenecks before they occur.

2. System Optimization: AI and ML can be used to automatically tune system performance. Instead of manual adjustments, intelligent systems can use ML algorithms to continually learn from system behavior and automatically adjust parameters to optimize performance.

3. Fraud Detection: Machine learning models can be trained to identify patterns that indicate fraudulent transactions. By analyzing numerous variables in real-time, these models can detect anomalies and potentially fraudulent activities with high accuracy, protecting both the business and its customers.

4. AI-driven Customer Experience: The transaction data stored in mainframes can be a goldmine of customer insights. AI can analyze these large volumes of data to understand customer behavior, preferences, and patterns, which can then be used to personalize customer

experiences and inform business strategies.

5. Automated Error Handling: AI can help in automatically detecting and diagnosing system errors, reducing downtime, and increasing system availability. ML models can be trained to recognize the symptoms of common problems and either resolve them automatically or suggest the most likely solutions to system administrators.

6. Natural Language Processing (NLP): NLP can be used in mainframe environments to help interpret and respond to user commands in natural language, making the system more accessible and easier to use.

As AI and ML continue to advance, their application in mainframe transaction processing is likely to grow. However, it's important to remember that these technologies need to be implemented thoughtfully, with considerations for data privacy and security, system performance, and the potential ethical implications of automated decision-making.

16.5 Security Advances

SECURITY CONTINUES to be a paramount concern for all IT systems, and mainframes, which handle a significant portion of the world's most sensitive data, are no exception. As threats evolve and become more sophisticated, so must the technologies and methodologies employed to defend against them. Some of the upcoming security advancements that may influence mainframe transaction processing include:

1. Quantum Computing and Cryptography: Quantum computers, when fully realized, pose a significant threat to current cryptographic methods because of their potential to crack encryption algorithms much faster than classical computers. In anticipation of this, research is already underway to develop quantum-resistant algorithms. This new form of cryptography, also known as post-quantum cryptography, is designed to secure data even in the era of quantum computers.

2. AI and ML for Security: Artificial Intelligence and Machine Learning can significantly enhance mainframe security. ML algorithms can analyze large volumes of data for anomalies that may indicate a security breach. Moreover, these algorithms can learn from each incident, improving their detection capabilities over time.

3. Behavioral Biometrics: This technology goes beyond traditional biometrics (like fingerprints or facial recognition) to analyze the unique ways a user interacts with a system. This could include keystroke dynamics, mouse movement patterns, or even the way a user types commands. Behavioral biometrics can provide an additional layer of security by continuously authenticating

users based on their interaction patterns.

4. Zero Trust Architectures: The zero trust model operates on the assumption that any user or system, whether inside or outside the network, could be a potential threat. This approach requires strict identity verification for every user and each device trying to access resources on a private network, regardless of whether they are sitting within or outside of the network perimeter. Zero trust can provide robust protection for mainframe data and resources.

5. Blockchain for Data Integrity: Blockchain technology, known for powering cryptocurrencies, can also enhance mainframe security. Blockchain can create immutable and verifiable logs of all transactions, ensuring data integrity and making it easier to detect unauthorized changes.

6. Privacy Enhancing Technologies (PETs): As data privacy regulations become more stringent worldwide, technologies that can help ensure privacy will become crucial. These include methods for anonymization, pseudonymization, differential privacy, and encrypted data processing.

While these advances hold significant potential, implementing them in the complex and often mission-critical world of mainframe transaction processing will require careful planning, testing, and consideration of potential trade-offs, especially those related to system performance and operational disruption.

16.6 Quantum Computing and Mainframes

QUANTUM COMPUTING REPRESENTS a significant leap forward in computation capabilities, offering potential for solving complex problems that are currently unfeasible for classical computers. Quantum computers operate on the principles of quantum mechanics, using quantum bits, or qubits, that can represent and manipulate a multitude of states at once, rather than just 0s and 1s.

The advent of quantum computing has profound implications for mainframe transaction processing in several ways:

1. Performance Improvement: Quantum computers, due to their inherent parallelism, could significantly speed up complex calculations and data analysis. They could potentially be used to process large volumes of transactions faster and more efficiently than classical computers.

2. Advanced Analytics: Quantum algorithms could enhance the ability of mainframes to perform advanced analytics. They could potentially sift through enormous datasets quickly and provide deep insights, thus improving decision-making processes in real-time transaction processing.

3. Enhanced Cryptography: Quantum computers could also enhance the security of mainframe systems. Quantum key distribution, for example, is a method that leverages the principles of quantum mechanics to provide secure communication. It makes eavesdropping virtually impossible and could play a crucial role in protecting data during transaction processing.

However, the potential of quantum computing also presents challenges:

1. Threat to Current Cryptography: Quantum computers have the theoretical ability to break many of the cryptographic algorithms currently in use, including those that secure mainframe data and transactions. This could force a complete rethinking of cryptographic approaches in mainframe environments.
2. Technological Maturity: As of my knowledge cutoff in September 2021, large-scale, fault-tolerant quantum computers have not yet been built. The technology is still in its infancy, and practical, widespread usage is likely still years away.
3. Integration with Existing Systems: Integrating quantum computing capabilities with existing mainframe systems is likely to be a complex task, involving significant architectural changes and potential disruption.

As the field of quantum computing advances, organizations will need to closely monitor developments and prepare for the potential advantages and challenges that this groundbreaking technology could bring to mainframe transaction processing.

16.7 Sustainability and Green Computing

AS THE GLOBAL FOCUS on environmental sustainability grows, so does the trend towards more energy-efficient and environmentally friendly computing technologies. This trend, often referred to as "green computing," has significant implications for the mainframe world, including transaction processing.

1. Energy Efficiency: Mainframes are already known for their high efficiency in terms of processing power per unit of energy consumed, compared to large clusters of smaller servers. However, there is a growing emphasis on improving this efficiency even further. This could involve more efficient power supplies, improved cooling technologies, and software optimizations that minimize power usage.

2. Data Center Design: Sustainability in data centers, where mainframes are often housed, is another key area of focus. This could involve the use of renewable energy sources, innovative cooling systems to reduce energy use, and the strategic location of data centers to take advantage of natural cooling options.

3. Reducing E-Waste: Mainframes' long operational life and scalability help reduce electronic waste (e-waste), as they do not need to be replaced as frequently as smaller servers. Additionally, recycling and responsible disposal programs for outdated hardware components are also an essential part of green computing initiatives.

4. Software and Processes: Green computing also extends to software and processing methods. Efficient algorithms reduce processing time and thus energy consumption. Furthermore, consolidation of applications and

virtualization can help optimize resource usage.

The trend towards sustainability and green computing has several implications for transaction processing:

1. Cost Savings: While the initial investment may be substantial, energy-efficient technologies can result in significant cost savings over the long term due to reduced energy bills.
2. Regulatory Compliance: Organizations are increasingly required to demonstrate that they are taking steps to reduce their environmental impact. Adopting green computing practices can help companies comply with these regulations.
3. Corporate Social Responsibility: Green computing initiatives can enhance an organization's reputation and align with corporate social responsibility goals.
4. Efficiency Improvements: Green initiatives often go hand-in-hand with efficiency improvements. For example, more efficient hardware or algorithms can not only reduce energy usage but also speed up transaction processing times.

As the IT industry continues to evolve, the focus on green computing is likely to become increasingly important. Therefore, understanding its implications for mainframe environments is crucial for organizations that depend on these systems for transaction processing.

16.8 Conclusion

THIS CHAPTER ON FUTURE trends in mainframe transaction processing has delved into the rapid evolution of mainframe technologies and how they continue to shape the world of transaction processing. From integration with cloud services to the harnessing of big data and artificial intelligence, mainframes remain at the cutting edge of technology, continually adapting and innovating.

The integration of mainframes with cloud-based technologies presents the opportunity for flexible, scalable, and cost-efficient computing solutions. The interoperability of these different environments is crucial for organizations that rely on the robustness of mainframes and the versatility of cloud services.

Big data and advanced analytics techniques, along with machine learning and artificial intelligence, are set to significantly influence transaction processing. These technologies allow for the extraction of meaningful insights, proactive error detection, and even automated optimization, making transaction processing more efficient and reliable.

Advancements in security continue to be a priority, with mainframes adopting new methods and technologies to ensure data integrity and confidentiality in transaction processing. The future may see even more sophisticated security measures, such as quantum-resistant cryptography.

Quantum computing, while still a developing field, holds the promise of dramatically increased processing power. Though its full implications for mainframes and transaction processing remain to be seen, it represents a fascinating direction for the future of computing.

Lastly, the emphasis on sustainability and green computing reflects the broader societal focus on environmental responsibility. The trend toward more energy-efficient and environmentally friendly technologies is influencing the design and operation of mainframes and the way transaction processing is carried out.

In conclusion, the world of mainframe transaction processing continues to evolve, influenced by advancements in technology and shifts in societal values and needs. Understanding these trends and adapting to them is crucial for organizations that want to maintain efficient, reliable, and secure transaction processing systems. As we continue to move forward, the resilience, adaptability, and robustness of mainframes will undoubtedly continue to serve as a cornerstone of global IT infrastructure.

Part VI: Practical Application and Case Studies

The final part of this book is focused on the practical application of the concepts, architectures, and strategies discussed in the previous sections. We will delve into the real-world aspect of implementing mainframe transaction processing, shedding light on the steps involved in setting up, configuring, and optimizing a mainframe environment for effective and efficient transaction processing.

Chapter 17: Implementing Mainframe Transaction Processing

This chapter provides a step-by-step guide on the implementation of mainframe transaction processing. It will take you through the planning phase, hardware and software selection, system configuration, application development, testing, and deployment stages. It will also cover essential factors such as performance tuning, security setup, and disaster recovery planning.

Chapter 18: Case Studies: Successful Implementations of Mainframe Transaction Processing

The final chapter presents several case studies that highlight successful implementations of mainframe transaction processing. These real-world examples, from various industries such as banking, insurance, and retail, provide valuable insights into how organizations have leveraged mainframe systems to handle massive transaction loads effectively and securely. These case studies not only illustrate the broad applicability of mainframe transaction processing but also offer practical lessons that can guide your own implementation journey.

Chapter 17: Implementing Mainframe Transaction Processing

17.1 Introduction: An overview of what this chapter entails, emphasizing the importance of practical implementation and the expected outcomes of the chapter.

17.2 Planning Phase: A detailed discussion on the initial steps involved in planning for mainframe transaction processing. This includes defining business needs, project scope, resource allocation, and developing a timeline.

17.3 Hardware and Software Selection: A guide on how to choose the right hardware and software for mainframe transaction processing, considering factors like transaction volume, data load, and specific business requirements.

17.4 System Configuration: This section provides instructions on how to set up and configure mainframe systems for transaction processing, covering areas like operating systems, databases, middleware, and network settings.

17.5 Application Development: An exploration of how to develop applications for mainframe transaction processing, discussing the role of programming languages, development tools, and methodologies.

17.6 Testing Phase: Here, we look at the importance of testing in the implementation process. This includes unit testing, integration testing, system testing, and performance testing.

17.7 Deployment and Go-live: This section covers the final steps of deploying the mainframe transaction processing system and transitioning it into live operation.

17.8 Performance Tuning and Optimization: A guide on how to monitor, tune, and optimize mainframe transaction processing for maximum performance and efficiency.

17.9 Security and Disaster Recovery Planning: This part focuses on the essential aspects of securing the mainframe environment and planning for disaster recovery.

17.10 Ongoing Maintenance and Support: A discussion on the strategies for maintaining the mainframe transaction processing environment and providing necessary support.

17.11 Conclusion: The chapter concludes with a summary of the key steps in implementing mainframe transaction processing, emphasizing the importance of meticulous planning, testing, and ongoing maintenance.

17.1 Introduction

THE ESSENCE OF THIS chapter is to highlight the practical aspects of implementing mainframe transaction processing systems. While a thorough understanding of theoretical concepts and architecture is necessary, the ability to translate this knowledge into practice is equally critical for successful application in the real world.

This chapter will walk you through the step-by-step process of implementing mainframe transaction processing, from initial planning stages to ongoing maintenance and support. We'll explore the importance of each phase, highlighting best practices, potential challenges, and key considerations to ensure a successful implementation.

The outcomes expected from this chapter are a firm understanding of the nuts and bolts of mainframe transaction processing implementation, the ability to navigate through its complexities, and the readiness to handle real-world challenges that may arise during the process.

Through this journey, we aim to empower you with the confidence and skills needed to effectively manage and oversee the implementation of mainframe transaction processing systems, ensuring they meet the specific needs of your organization while offering optimal performance and security.

17.2 Planning Phase

THE INITIAL PLANNING phase is crucial in any implementation process, including that of mainframe transaction processing. During this phase, several key aspects are defined and laid out to ensure the smooth execution of the project.

1. Defining Business Needs: Understanding and defining business needs is the first step in planning. It involves understanding the business requirements that the system needs to address, such as the volume of transactions to be processed, the need for real-time processing, regulatory compliance requirements, and so on.

2. Project Scope: The next step is defining the project scope. This involves identifying the specific capabilities that the mainframe transaction processing system should have to meet the identified business needs. It may also involve determining the boundaries of the project, such as which departments or business functions will be impacted and to what extent.

3. Resource Allocation: Resource allocation involves identifying the resources needed to implement the project. This includes personnel, hardware and software resources, and financial resources. It also involves assigning roles and responsibilities to team members.

4. Developing a Timeline: The timeline for the implementation project is also developed during the planning phase. This involves setting deadlines for each stage of the project and developing a schedule that details when each task should be started and completed.

A well-executed planning phase helps in setting clear goals and objectives for the project, ensures efficient use of resources, and paves the way for a successful implementation. It's important to remember that the planning phase is iterative and might need revisions as the project progresses and more details come to light.

17.3 Hardware and Software Selection

MAKING THE RIGHT HARDWARE and software choices for mainframe transaction processing is crucial for effective and efficient system performance.

1. Transaction Volume: The volume of transactions that a mainframe needs to handle is one of the most important factors to consider. Larger volumes necessitate more powerful and efficient systems. Consideration needs to be given to peak transaction periods to ensure that the system does not falter under heavy load.
2. Data Load: The size of the data that needs to be processed and stored is another key factor. Larger data sets may require more storage capacity, faster disk speeds, and potentially more memory to hold and process data. Mainframe hardware should be chosen with enough capacity to handle expected data growth over time.
3. Business Requirements: Specific business requirements also dictate hardware and software selection. For instance, certain industries might require real-time transaction processing, necessitating high-speed processors and low-latency network connections. Regulatory requirements might also mandate specific data security or redundancy features.
4. Software Considerations: Software choices for mainframe systems include the operating system, database management systems (DBMS), transaction processing monitors, and middleware. Each of these choices should align with the system's intended purpose, expected workload, and user needs. For instance, the chosen DBMS should support the expected transaction rate and type of

transactions (e.g., OLTP or batch processing).

5. Vendor Support and Community: Choosing hardware and software from vendors with strong support services is crucial for long-term system maintenance and troubleshooting. Also, a large user community can be a great resource for solving problems and getting advice on best practices.

The process of hardware and software selection should involve careful consideration, research, and, ideally, consultation with experts or experienced professionals in the field. It's also important to remember that both hardware and software should be scalable to handle future growth or changes in business requirements.

17.4 System Configuration

CONFIGURING A MAINFRAME system for transaction processing involves several key steps across different areas:

1. Operating System Configuration: The operating system (OS) is the foundation on which all other software runs. Configuration at this level involves setting up user accounts, permissions, and security policies. Depending on the specific OS, there may also be system parameters that can be tuned to optimize performance for transaction processing workloads.

2. Database Configuration: The database configuration is critical for efficient transaction processing. This can include defining schemas, setting up tables, tuning database parameters for performance, setting up indexes, and configuring backup and recovery procedures. Proper normalization and use of indexing can significantly impact the speed of transactions.

3. Middleware Configuration: Middleware such as transaction processing monitors or message-oriented middleware needs to be configured to handle transactional workloads. This could include setting up communication protocols, message queues, transaction timeout values, and other parameters.

4. Network Configuration: The network configuration should be optimized to ensure fast and reliable communication between the mainframe and other systems. This may involve setting up routers and switches, configuring firewalls, and setting up network protocols.

5. Security Configuration: This involves setting up encryption for data at rest and in transit, configuring access

controls, setting up audit logs, and integrating with enterprise security systems if necessary.

6. Performance Tuning: After the initial configuration, performance tuning may be necessary. This can involve adjusting system parameters, reorganizing databases, or modifying application code to optimize performance. This is often an iterative process that involves monitoring system performance, identifying bottlenecks, making adjustments, and then re-evaluating performance.

7. Regular Maintenance: After the system is set up and running, regular maintenance tasks are essential to ensure continued optimal performance and security. This can include patching software, checking and optimizing database performance, reviewing security logs, and so on.

Overall, system configuration for mainframe transaction processing is a complex task that requires a deep understanding of the hardware, software, and the specific workload requirements. It's often a collaborative effort involving system administrators, database administrators, and application developers.

17.5 Application Development

DEVELOPING APPLICATIONS for mainframe transaction processing is a specialized task that requires a deep understanding of both mainframe systems and transaction processing concepts. The key aspects that are typically involved in this process are:

1. Programming Languages: Mainframe applications can be written in a variety of languages, including COBOL, Java, C/C++, and newer languages such as Python. The choice of language will depend on a variety of factors, including the specific requirements of the application, the skills of the development team, and the mainframe environment. For example, COBOL is traditionally used for business applications due to its excellent processing speed and close integration with mainframe systems, while Java might be chosen for its object-oriented features and broad ecosystem of libraries and frameworks.

2. Development Tools: There are a variety of tools available for mainframe application development. These can include Integrated Development Environments (IDEs) that support mainframe languages, debuggers, version control systems, and testing tools. For example, IBM's z/OS Explorer and Compuware's Topaz are popular tools for developing mainframe applications.

3. Methodologies: Mainframe application development can use a variety of methodologies, including traditional Waterfall development, Agile, DevOps, and others. The choice of methodology can depend on factors such as the size and complexity of the project, the organization's culture, and the need for flexibility and rapid feedback. Regardless of the methodology chosen, it's important to

include best practices such as code reviews, automated testing, and continuous integration to ensure the quality of the application.

4. Designing for Transaction Processing: Designing applications for transaction processing requires an understanding of concepts such as ACID properties (Atomicity, Consistency, Isolation, Durability), concurrency control, and error handling. Applications should be designed to minimize contention for resources, handle errors gracefully, and ensure data integrity even in the event of system failures.

5. Testing and Performance Tuning: Once the application has been developed, it should be thoroughly tested to ensure it meets the required functional and performance requirements. This can involve unit testing, integration testing, system testing, and performance testing. Performance tuning can involve optimizing database queries, adjusting concurrency control mechanisms, and optimizing the application code itself.

Overall, developing applications for mainframe transaction processing is a critical task that requires specialized skills and knowledge. It's an area where experience and deep understanding of mainframe systems can make a significant difference to the success of a project.

17.6 Testing Phase

TESTING IS A CRITICAL part of the implementation process for mainframe transaction processing. The goal of testing is to ensure that the system functions as expected under a variety of conditions and to identify any bugs or performance issues. There are several types of testing that are typically performed:

1. Unit Testing: This is the first level of testing, where individual components (like functions or methods within a program) are tested in isolation. The goal is to confirm that each component behaves as expected according to its design and requirements. For example, a unit test might verify that a function correctly updates a database record in response to a specific input.

2. Integration Testing: Once individual components have been unit tested, they are combined and tested together in integration testing. This is designed to catch issues that arise from the interaction between different components, such as data inconsistencies or synchronization problems. For example, an integration test might verify that a sequence of transactions correctly updates multiple related database records.

3. System Testing: This is a high-level test that validates the system as a whole, ensuring that it meets all specified requirements. System testing typically involves a wide range of scenarios, including both normal operation and error conditions. For example, a system test might verify that the transaction processing system can handle a high volume of transactions without slowing down or crashing.

4. Performance Testing: This is a specialized form of testing designed to evaluate the system's performance

characteristics, such as processing speed, response times, and throughput. Performance testing is critical for mainframe transaction processing systems, which often need to handle very high transaction volumes. Performance testing can help identify bottlenecks and performance issues, allowing them to be addressed before the system goes live.

5. Regression Testing: This testing is performed after modifications in the system or its components to ensure that existing functionality still works as expected and no new bugs have been introduced. Regression testing can be a part of each of the above stages.

6. Acceptance Testing: This is usually the final phase of testing, performed by end-users or clients to validate the system against business requirements. If the system passes acceptance testing, it can be considered ready for production use.

Each of these testing phases plays a crucial role in ensuring that the mainframe transaction processing system is reliable, efficient, and accurate. By thoroughly testing the system at each stage of development, organizations can avoid costly and disruptive issues once the system is live.

17.7 Deployment and Go-live

THE DEPLOYMENT PHASE is the final step in the implementation of a mainframe transaction processing system. This involves the transfer of all components, applications, and databases from the development or staging environment to the production environment. Here, it's crucial to have a solid deployment plan in place to avoid disruptions to business operations. This section of the chapter covers the key aspects of this process:

1. Deployment Planning: Deployment involves careful planning to ensure a smooth transition to the live environment. This planning process includes determining the ideal time for deployment (usually during off-peak hours), assigning responsibilities to the team members, and creating a detailed deployment schedule.

2. Data Migration: If applicable, existing data may need to be migrated from an old system to the new mainframe system. This is a delicate process that needs to be carefully managed to prevent data loss or corruption. It may involve data cleaning, data transformation, and careful validation to ensure that all data has been accurately transferred.

3. System Setup: Deployment includes setting up the system in the production environment. This includes configuring hardware and software, establishing network connections, installing and configuring applications, and setting up databases.

4. Final Testing: Once the system is set up, a final round of testing is typically conducted in the production environment. This helps to ensure that the system operates as expected in its live setting. It may include acceptance testing, performance testing, and security testing.

5. Transition to Operations: Once testing is complete and the system is confirmed to be working correctly, the system can go live. This involves transitioning all operations from the old system (if one exists) to the new mainframe transaction processing system.

6. Training and Support: To ensure a smooth transition, end users and system operators may need training on how to use the new system. This could involve on-site training sessions, user manuals, or online tutorials. It's also important to have a support structure in place to help users troubleshoot any issues they might encounter.

7. Monitoring and Adjustment: After the system goes live, it should be continuously monitored to ensure it's working as expected. This will involve regular checks of system performance, as well as monitoring for any potential issues or errors. As the system is used, there may be a need for adjustments or enhancements based on user feedback or observed performance.

The "Go-live" stage is a critical point in the lifecycle of a mainframe transaction processing system. A successful go-live can signal a period of enhanced productivity and operational efficiency, while issues during this phase can lead to operational disruptions and loss of confidence in the new system. As such, it's essential to approach this stage with a well-defined plan, clear communication, and a strong understanding of the system and its operation.

17.8 Performance Tuning and Optimization

ONCE A MAINFRAME TRANSACTION processing system has been implemented and is in operation, the work doesn't stop there. To ensure the system operates at its peak performance, regular monitoring, tuning, and optimization activities are necessary. This section of the chapter explores these concepts in greater detail:

1. Performance Monitoring: This involves regularly checking key performance metrics such as CPU usage, memory utilization, I/O operations, transaction throughput, and response times. Specialized monitoring tools may be used to track these metrics over time, generate reports, and trigger alerts when certain thresholds are breached.

2. Performance Analysis: After collecting performance data, it's necessary to analyze it to identify any potential issues or bottlenecks. For example, high CPU usage might indicate inefficient application code, while long response times might point to network latency or slow disk I/O.

3. Benchmarking: Benchmarking involves comparing your system's performance against a standard or set of predefined criteria. This could be performance metrics from a previous system, industry standards, or objectives set during the planning phase.

4. Tuning and Optimization: Based on the insights gained from performance monitoring and analysis, specific tuning and optimization measures can be taken. This could involve tweaking system settings, optimizing database queries, improving application code, or even upgrading hardware. The goal is to improve the system's efficiency, reduce resource usage, and improve transaction processing times.

5. Capacity Planning: This is a proactive strategy that involves predicting future system loads and ensuring the mainframe system can handle this load. This may involve scaling up (adding more resources to the system) or scaling out (adding more systems).

6. Continual Improvement: Performance tuning and optimization is not a one-time activity, but an ongoing process. As the system load changes and as new performance data is collected, further adjustments and improvements may be necessary.

Performance tuning and optimization is an integral part of managing a mainframe transaction processing system. It helps ensure that the system can handle the demands of its users efficiently and reliably, and that it makes effective use of system resources. Not only does this lead to better system performance, but it can also result in significant cost savings over the long term.

17.9 Security and Disaster Recovery Planning

IMPLEMENTING A MAINFRAME transaction processing system involves not only setting up the necessary hardware, software, and applications, but also ensuring that the system is secure and resilient. This part of the chapter discusses these crucial aspects in detail:

1. Security Planning: Mainframes often handle sensitive data and business-critical operations, making them attractive targets for cyber-attacks. As such, security should be a top priority from the outset. This involves:
    ◦ Access Control: Defining who can access the system, and what they can do. This includes setting up user accounts, roles, and permissions.
    ◦ Data Security: Ensuring that data stored and processed on the mainframe is protected. This includes measures such as encryption, data masking, and secure data disposal.
    ◦ Network Security: Protecting the network connections to and from the mainframe. This may involve setting up firewalls, intrusion detection systems, and secure communication protocols.
    ◦ Security Monitoring and Incident Response: Implementing mechanisms to detect and respond to security incidents. This can involve security information and event management (SIEM) systems, and developing an incident response plan.
2. Disaster Recovery Planning: No system is immune to failures, be it due to hardware faults, software bugs, human errors, or external factors like natural disasters. Therefore,

it's essential to have a disaster recovery plan in place:

- ○ Backup and Restore: Regular backups should be made of all critical data. It's also necessary to ensure that this data can be restored successfully.
- ○ Redundancy: Key hardware and network components can be duplicated to ensure that if one fails, the system can continue to operate.
- ○ Failover: In the event of a system failure, operations can be switched over to a standby system.
- ○ Disaster Recovery Testing: The disaster recovery plan should be tested regularly to ensure that it works as expected. This might involve drills or simulations of disaster scenarios.

Security and disaster recovery planning are not just about protecting against threats and failures. They are about ensuring the continuity and reliability of mainframe transaction processing, which can have a direct impact on the organization's operations and reputation.

17.10 Ongoing Maintenance and Support

AFTER THE MAINFRAME transaction processing system has been deployed and is live, the work is not done. The system needs to be maintained and supported to ensure it remains operational, efficient, and secure. This section of the chapter discusses these ongoing tasks:

1. Software Updates and Patches: It's crucial to keep all system software, including the operating system, middleware, database systems, and application software, up to date. Updates often include bug fixes, performance improvements, and security patches that can protect the system against known vulnerabilities. A process should be in place to regularly check for and install updates, taking care to test them in a separate environment first to avoid disruptions.

2. Hardware Maintenance: Over time, hardware can degrade or become obsolete. Regular hardware maintenance can help detect and prevent potential failures. This includes tasks like cleaning and inspecting hardware, monitoring hardware health and performance, and upgrading or replacing hardware as needed.

3. Performance Monitoring and Tuning: System performance should be continually monitored to identify any issues or inefficiencies. Performance data can also help identify trends and plan for future capacity needs. If performance issues are detected, the system may need to be tuned or optimized.

4. Backup and Recovery: Regular backups should continue to be made to protect against data loss. Backup processes should be monitored to ensure they are completing

successfully, and recovery procedures should be tested regularly.

5. User Support: Users of the system may need ongoing support. This can include training on system use, assistance with problems or errors, and updates on any changes or interruptions to service.

6. Security Monitoring: Continual monitoring for security threats is crucial. This can involve reviewing security logs, running vulnerability scans, and keeping abreast of new security threats and vulnerabilities.

7. Documentation and Change Management: Keeping documentation up to date is crucial for ongoing operations and for handling unexpected incidents or changes in personnel. Any changes to the system or its operation should be carefully managed and documented to ensure system stability and minimize disruptions.

Ongoing maintenance and support require dedicated resources, but they are vital for keeping the mainframe transaction processing system functional, efficient, secure, and able to meet the organization's changing needs.

17.11 Conclusion

17.11 CONCLUSION: IMPLEMENTING mainframe transaction processing systems is a significant task, requiring careful planning, execution, and ongoing management. However, these systems are crucial for handling large-scale, complex transaction processing needs, and their successful implementation can significantly enhance an organization's operational efficiency and capability.

This chapter walked the readers through the entire process, from initial planning and hardware and software selection, to configuration, application development, testing, and deployment. We stressed the importance of comprehensive testing at each stage of the development process to ensure that the system is ready for the rigors of live operation.

We also underscored the necessity of proper performance tuning and optimization to ensure that your mainframe transaction processing system delivers the highest levels of performance and efficiency. Security considerations and disaster recovery planning were highlighted as critical components of any implementation strategy, protecting the integrity of transactions and continuity of business operations.

Lastly, we discussed the critical nature of ongoing maintenance and support, emphasizing that the implementation process does not end once the system goes live. Ongoing software updates, hardware maintenance, performance monitoring, user support, and security monitoring are all vital for the continued success and reliability of the system.

In conclusion, while implementing mainframe transaction processing can be complex, with the right strategy, meticulous planning, and careful execution, it's a task that can significantly enhance the capability and efficiency of an organization. As technology continues to evolve, understanding these processes will be increasingly important for managing transaction processing at scale.

Chapter 18: Case Studies: Successful Implementations of Mainframe Transaction Processing

18.1 Introduction: This chapter presents various real-world case studies that demonstrate successful implementations of mainframe transaction processing. These case studies are intended to provide practical insights and lessons learned from organizations that have successfully navigated the complexities of implementing and maintaining these systems.

18.2 Case Study 1: This section presents a detailed case study of a large financial institution that successfully implemented mainframe transaction processing to manage its high-volume, high-speed transaction needs. It delves into the planning, implementation, and maintenance stages, highlighting the specific challenges encountered and solutions applied.

18.3 Case Study 2: This part discusses another case study, this time from the retail sector, where a global retailer used mainframe transaction processing to streamline its inventory management and sales processes. It showcases how the company integrated mainframe systems with modern technologies for a seamless, efficient transaction processing system.

18.4 Case Study 3: Here, a case study from the healthcare industry is presented, demonstrating how a large healthcare provider leveraged mainframe transaction processing to handle massive patient data and complex transactions. It emphasizes the role of data security and privacy considerations in the implementation process.

18.5 Case Study 4: This section looks at a government agency's implementation of mainframe transaction processing to handle citizen services and internal operations. It highlights the agency's approach to security, scalability, and the integration of legacy systems.

18.6 Comparative Analysis: This part provides a comparative analysis of the case studies, identifying common challenges, solutions, and successful strategies. It offers readers valuable insights that can inform their own mainframe transaction processing implementations.

18.7 Lessons Learned: This section distills the key lessons learned from the case studies, offering practical tips and guidance for organizations planning to implement their own mainframe transaction processing systems.

18.8 Conclusion: The chapter concludes with a reflection on the significance of these case studies and the value of learning from the experiences of other organizations. It emphasizes the continued relevance of mainframe transaction processing in today's tech landscape and its potential for the future.

18.1 Introduction

THE INTRODUCTION TO Chapter 18 sets the stage for the exploration of a variety of real-world case studies showcasing successful implementations of mainframe transaction processing. The goal of this chapter is to present practical, tangible examples of how different organizations, across a range of industries, have leveraged mainframe technology to handle their transaction processing needs.

Understanding the application of theoretical concepts in practical scenarios is a crucial part of learning and this chapter aims to bridge that gap. These case studies will not only provide insights into the process of implementing and maintaining mainframe transaction processing systems, but also highlight the unique challenges each organization faced and how they overcame them.

These case studies could involve various sectors such as finance, retail, healthcare, or government, each with its unique set of requirements and constraints. By studying these examples, readers will be able to gain a comprehensive understanding of the versatility and robustness of mainframe systems in handling diverse transaction processing needs.

The case studies may include details such as the initial situation or problem the organization faced, the planning and decision-making process they followed, how they implemented the solution, and how they dealt with any challenges or issues that arose. They will also discuss the outcomes of these implementations, including the benefits realized and lessons learned.

Ultimately, the aim is for readers to take away valuable lessons from these case studies that can inform their own approach to implementing and managing mainframe transaction processing systems.

18.2 Case Study 1

IN THE FIRST CASE STUDY, we look at a large financial institution that successfully deployed mainframe transaction processing to manage its vast and high-speed transaction needs.

The financial institution, due to the nature of its business, had a critical requirement to process high volumes of transactions reliably and securely. Moreover, due to regulatory requirements and the high stakes involved, the transactions needed to be processed quickly and without error.

During the planning stage, the institution outlined its transaction requirements, identifying peak transaction periods, necessary security measures, and expected growth over time. They also identified the hardware and software needs, deciding on a mainframe solution known for its reliability, scalability, and robust security features.

The implementation stage involved setting up the mainframe system, configuring it for their specific needs, and developing the necessary applications for transaction processing. This was a complex process, involving collaboration between various teams within the organization. A significant challenge was the need to migrate from their existing system to the new mainframe system without disrupting daily operations.

To address this challenge, the institution adopted a phased approach, first implementing the mainframe system in a testing environment, and then gradually migrating functions while the old and new systems ran in parallel. This allowed them to troubleshoot and resolve issues without impacting their day-to-day operations.

During the maintenance stage, the institution faced the challenge of ensuring system performance and reliability while also dealing with increasing transaction volumes over time. They tackled this with proactive system monitoring, regular performance tuning, and capacity planning for future growth.

The institution's implementation of mainframe transaction processing was successful, resulting in faster transaction processing times, higher system availability, and improved security. The case study concludes by highlighting the lessons learned, emphasizing the importance of careful planning, cross-team collaboration, and proactive system maintenance.

18.3 Case Study 2

IN THIS CASE STUDY, we turn our focus to a global retailer that used mainframe transaction processing to streamline its inventory management and sales processes. The unique challenge here was the need to handle not only high volumes of transactions but also to integrate mainframe systems with modern technologies for a seamless, efficient transaction processing system.

The retailer operates hundreds of stores worldwide, each carrying thousands of individual items. They needed a system that could handle the vast amounts of transaction data generated daily and also integrate this data in real-time with their inventory management system.

The planning stage was especially crucial. They needed to understand the precise nature of their requirements, identifying peak transaction times, specific data needs, and the requirement for real-time data processing. They also had to consider the need to interface their mainframe with modern technologies used in their stores, including point-of-sale systems, mobile devices, and e-commerce platforms.

During the implementation stage, they adopted a mainframe solution renowned for its processing capabilities, reliability, and capacity to integrate with different technologies. An agile development methodology was employed, allowing the implementation team to adapt the system according to emerging requirements. A key challenge was ensuring seamless data flow between the mainframe and the different technologies used in stores. This was achieved by leveraging middleware solutions and implementing robust APIs.

To ensure smooth operation and high performance, the retailer implemented regular performance monitoring and tuning. They also implemented stringent security measures, given the sensitivity of customer transaction data.

The implementation was a success, leading to streamlined operations, better inventory management, and improved customer experience due to real-time data processing. The case study concludes by highlighting the power of mainframes when integrated with modern technologies and emphasizes the importance of flexibility and adaptability in implementing mainframe transaction processing systems.

18.4 Case Study 3

IN THIS CASE STUDY, we delve into the healthcare industry, specifically examining how a large healthcare provider leveraged mainframe transaction processing to handle its enormous amounts of patient data and complex transactions. This implementation not only had to prioritize efficiency and reliability but also had to put data security and privacy at the forefront due to the sensitive nature of health-related information.

The healthcare provider in this study operates multiple hospitals and clinics, each generating vast amounts of patient data every day. This data not only includes medical information but also administrative details such as billing and insurance claims, all of which require efficient processing. Furthermore, stringent regulations, such as the Health Insurance Portability and Accountability Act (HIPAA) in the U.S., mandated a high level of security and privacy for patient data.

During the planning phase, the provider identified the need for a robust mainframe system that could handle high volumes of complex transactions, while also having top-notch security features. They also identified the need for integration with various healthcare information systems used across their facilities.

In the implementation phase, they opted for a mainframe system known for its high processing power, reliability, and advanced security features. A key challenge was integrating the mainframe with existing healthcare information systems. They solved this by developing custom interfaces using middleware solutions, ensuring seamless data flow between systems.

On the security front, they implemented encryption for data at rest and in transit, role-based access control, and regular security audits. They also planned for disaster recovery to ensure data integrity and availability even in case of emergencies.

The system's go-live phase saw the successful implementation of mainframe transaction processing, which improved efficiency in handling patient data and processing transactions. It also ensured top-tier security and privacy for patient data.

This case study demonstrates the flexibility and robustness of mainframe transaction processing systems when used in highly regulated environments that deal with sensitive data. It underlines the importance of careful planning, especially around system security and privacy, and the need for effective integration with existing systems.

18.5 Case Study 4

IN THIS CASE STUDY, we look at how a government agency used mainframe transaction processing to handle citizen services and internal operations. Government agencies pose a unique set of challenges due to their wide range of services, large user base, and stringent security requirements. Furthermore, such agencies often have legacy systems in place, which need to be carefully integrated or replaced.

The government agency in this case study provides a wide range of services to citizens, from tax collection to social services. They deal with a high volume of transactions, many of which are time-sensitive. The agency also has a significant amount of historical data stored in legacy systems.

During the planning phase, the agency prioritized security, scalability, and the integration of legacy systems. They needed a system that could handle a large increase in transactions, especially during peak periods such as tax season. The agency also required the system to have robust security features to protect sensitive personal data of citizens.

When choosing the hardware and software, the agency opted for a mainframe system known for its high transaction processing capabilities and advanced security features. They also selected software that could seamlessly integrate with their legacy systems.

During the system configuration and application development phase, the agency faced challenges due to the age and complexity of their legacy systems. However, with careful planning and the use of middleware, they were able to integrate these systems successfully.

In terms of security, the agency implemented measures such as encryption, two-factor authentication, and regular security audits. They also developed a comprehensive disaster recovery plan to ensure continuity of services in case of emergencies.

Once the system was live, the agency saw a significant improvement in transaction processing speed, even during peak periods. They were also able to achieve a high level of security, ensuring the privacy of citizens' data. The integration with legacy systems ensured that historical data was still accessible and usable.

This case study demonstrates the efficacy of mainframe transaction processing in a complex, high-demand environment. It underscores the need for careful planning, especially when dealing with legacy systems, and the importance of security when handling sensitive data.

18.6 Comparative Analysis

IN THIS SECTION, WE examine the commonalities and differences among the four case studies presented. This comparative analysis highlights shared challenges, effective solutions, and successful strategies that can be drawn from the various contexts of financial services, retail, healthcare, and government. This knowledge can guide readers in implementing mainframe transaction processing in their own organizations.

1. Common Challenges: Each case study demonstrated unique challenges based on the sector they operate in. However, common challenges include integrating with existing legacy systems, ensuring robust security, managing high-volume transactions, and planning for scalability. Additionally, the need for meticulous planning and efficient project management was evident in all cases.

2. Effective Solutions: Solutions varied depending on the specific challenges faced. However, the use of middleware was a common theme for integration with legacy systems. Robust security measures, including encryption, two-factor authentication, and regular security audits, were implemented across all sectors. To manage high-volume transactions and ensure scalability, all organizations opted for high-capacity mainframe systems.

3. Successful Strategies: Despite the differences in implementation, several successful strategies emerged. Proactive planning, including detailed project scope, resource allocation, and timelines, was a shared strategy. Rigorous testing during the implementation phase was another common success factor. All organizations also emphasized the importance of ongoing maintenance and

support, with an emphasis on security and performance tuning.

This comparative analysis provides important insights into the real-world application of mainframe transaction processing. Despite differences in sector and scope, the importance of careful planning, robust security, integration strategies, and ongoing maintenance are applicable to all organizations considering similar implementations.

18.7 Lessons Learned

THIS PART OF THE CHAPTER distills the key insights and lessons learned from the previous case studies. These lessons can guide organizations in planning and implementing their own mainframe transaction processing systems:

1. Thorough Planning is Key: The successful implementation of a mainframe transaction processing system begins with detailed and careful planning. This includes clearly defining business requirements, establishing a realistic project scope, and allocating resources effectively.

2. Integration with Legacy Systems: Integrating the new system with existing legacy systems can be challenging. It's crucial to consider compatibility and integration requirements early in the planning process and to use middleware solutions where appropriate.

3. Importance of Robust Security Measures: The case studies highlighted the critical role of robust security measures in mainframe transaction processing. This involves implementing secure access controls, data encryption, regular security audits, and following best practices for data security and privacy.

4. Managing High-Volume Transactions: All the case studies emphasized the need for mainframe systems that can handle high-volume transactions effectively. This requires careful capacity planning and selecting the right hardware and software solutions.

5. Scalability Considerations: Mainframe systems should be designed with scalability in mind to handle future growth in transaction volumes. This involves proactive capacity planning and choosing scalable technologies.

6. Testing and Performance Tuning: Rigorous testing at various stages of the implementation process is vital to detect and rectify any issues. Regular performance tuning after the system goes live can help ensure the system continues to operate efficiently.

7. Continuous Maintenance and Support: Continuous system maintenance and support are necessary for smooth operations. This includes monitoring system performance, updating software components, handling user queries, and troubleshooting any issues that arise.

8. Disaster Recovery Planning: Implementing a comprehensive disaster recovery plan can help safeguard your mainframe systems and data in the event of a system failure or other unforeseen incidents.

These lessons learned provide valuable guidance that can help organizations avoid common pitfalls and ensure a successful implementation of their mainframe transaction processing systems.

18.8 Conclusion

THIS SECTION WRAPS up the chapter by highlighting the key takeaways from the case studies presented and reflecting on their broader implications.

Learning from the experiences of other organizations that have successfully implemented mainframe transaction processing systems can provide valuable insights. Each case study, from different sectors including finance, retail, healthcare, and government, highlighted the versatile use cases of mainframe transaction processing systems, demonstrating their capability to handle high-volume, complex transactions securely and efficiently.

The mainframe, a technology that has been around for several decades, continues to play a significant role in today's digital landscape, particularly in scenarios where high performance, robust security, and reliable transaction processing are required. The case studies underscore the importance of meticulous planning, effective system integration, comprehensive testing, continuous performance tuning, and diligent security measures, all of which contribute to the successful implementation and operation of these systems.

Looking forward, as the volume of digital transactions continues to grow and as technological advances are made, mainframe transaction processing systems are likely to evolve and adapt to new requirements. As such, the lessons learned from these case studies will continue to be relevant for organizations that rely on mainframes for their transaction processing needs.

In conclusion, while the technology landscape is ever-evolving, the key principles and practices for implementing and managing mainframe transaction processing systems remain consistent. A thoughtful approach to planning, implementation, and maintenance, as demonstrated by these case studies, can ensure the success and longevity of such systems.

Part VII: Appendices

———

This final part of the book serves as a useful reference and a guide to further learning. It includes a glossary of key terms and concepts related to mainframe transaction processing, as well as a list of additional resources for readers who want to delve deeper into specific topics.

Appendix A: Glossary of Mainframe Transaction Processing Terms

This appendix is a comprehensive glossary of terms related to mainframe transaction processing. It aims to provide clear definitions and explanations of key concepts, acronyms, and jargon used throughout the book. This glossary serves as a quick reference guide, aiding in the understanding of complex technical terminology and enhancing readers' comprehension of the subject matter.

Appendix B: Additional Resources

This appendix presents a list of additional resources, including books, research papers, articles, and online courses related to mainframe transaction processing. These resources have been carefully curated to provide readers with opportunities for deeper exploration of the topics covered in this book. These references also include resources for keeping up-to-date with emerging trends and technologies in mainframe transaction processing, allowing readers to continually expand their knowledge and stay current in this rapidly evolving field.

Appendix A: Glossary of Mainframe Transaction Processing Terms

This appendix offers an alphabetical listing of the key terms, concepts, and acronyms related to mainframe transaction processing. Some example entries might include:

1. ACID (Atomicity, Consistency, Isolation, Durability): A set of properties that guarantee database transactions are processed reliably in a system.
2. Batch Processing: A method of processing high volumes of data where a group of transactions is collected over time and then processed all at once.
3. Concurrency: The execution of multiple transactions in overlapping time intervals, aimed at improving system efficiency.
4. Deadlock: A state where two or more processes are unable to proceed because each is waiting for the other to release a resource.
5. Mainframe: A large, powerful computer system, capable of processing and managing much larger amounts of data compared to other computers. They are used mainly by large organizations for critical applications, typically bulk data processing.
6. Middleware: Software that provides services to applications beyond those provided by the operating system to enable interoperability.
7. Real-Time Processing: The processing of database transactions that are received in a continuous (real-time) flow and are processed as soon as they are received.

8. Transaction Processing System (TPS): A type of system, typically a software application, where the computational task is the processing of transactions.

9. Two-Phase Commit Protocol: A protocol that ensures all parties in a distributed system agree to commit a transaction or abort (rollback) the transaction if a failure occurs.

10. z/OS: An operating system for IBM mainframes, designed for enterprise-level applications requiring high reliability and maximum levels of availability.

These are just a few examples. The glossary would contain many more terms and definitions that are relevant to the subject matter covered in the book.

Appendix B: Additional Resources

This appendix provides a compilation of additional resources that readers can explore to further their understanding of mainframe transaction processing. These resources can include books, research papers, online courses, websites, forums, and software tools. Below are a few examples:

Books:

1. "Introduction to the New Mainframe: z/OS Basics" by IBM Redbooks: A comprehensive introduction to the mainframe world.
2. "Mainframes: Basic Concepts and Design Principles" by N. G. Prasad: Offers a fundamental understanding of mainframes and their design principles.

Research Papers:

1. "Transaction Processing: Concepts and Techniques" by Jim Gray and Andreas Reuter: A comprehensive reference on transaction processing systems.

Online Courses:

1. IBM's 'Introduction to z/OS and the Mainframe Environment': A beginner's course provided by IBM on Coursera.
2. 'Mainframe: The Complete COBOL Course From Beginner To Expert': A comprehensive Udemy course on COBOL, a core mainframe programming language.

Websites/Forums:

1. IBM Developer Community: A platform for developers to collaborate, share knowledge, and learn from experts.
2. Mainframe Watch Belgium: A blog that provides news, tips, and insights into the world of mainframes.

Software Tools:

1. IBM Z: IBM's family of mainframe servers.
2. z/OS: The operating system for IBM's mainframe computers.

Remember, the actual list of resources would be much more extensive and cover a wide array of topics related to mainframe transaction processing. It's always a good idea to keep yourself updated with the latest resources, as the world of mainframes and transaction processing is constantly evolving.

Epilogue

In our journey through the world of mainframe transaction processing, we have covered a wide range of topics - from basic concepts to advanced transactional models, from implementation strategies to future trends. This book has strived to provide a comprehensive understanding of this critical technology that continues to power some of the world's most complex, data-intensive operations.

However, the landscape of information technology is ever-evolving, with innovations and advancements continuously changing the game. The future of mainframes and transaction processing is poised to adapt to these changes, integrating with emerging technologies like cloud computing, artificial intelligence, big data, and potentially even quantum computing.

As we conclude this book, it's crucial to remember that learning is a continuous process. The information, insights, and strategies presented here provide a strong foundation, but there is always more to explore and understand.

We hope that this book has sparked your interest in mainframe transaction processing and has equipped you with the knowledge and tools to succeed in this exciting field. Whether you're a student, a professional, a researcher, or simply an enthusiast, remember that your journey doesn't end here. Keep learning, keep exploring, and keep pushing the boundaries of what's possible in the world of mainframe transaction processing.

Thank you for joining us on this journey, and we look forward to seeing how you contribute to the future of mainframes.

Don't miss out!

Visit the website below and you can sign up to receive emails whenever Ricardo Nuqui publishes a new book. There's no charge and no obligation.

https://books2read.com/r/B-A-EXMX-PHGKC

Connecting independent readers to independent writers.

Did you love *Mainframe Transaction Processing: Principles, Practices, and Paradigms*? Then you should read *Harnessing Mainframe Databases: Strategies for Modern Data Management*[1] by Ricardo Nuqui!

Harnessing Mainframe Databases:
Strategies for Modern Data Management [2]

This book, "Harnessing Mainframe Databases: Strategies for Modern Data Management," was born out of the need for a comprehensive and up-to-date resource on mainframe databases. It is intended to help both novices and seasoned IT professionals navigate the complex landscape of these unique data systems.

Starting with an introduction to the world of mainframes and their databases, we delve into the intricate details of their architecture, data management, and performance optimization. We dedicate substantial sections to explore key technologies, such as

---

IMS, DB2, VSAM, and IDMS, among others. The aim is not only to understand these systems but also to get hands-on with their practical aspects, including security, data integration, and ETL processes.

The book also looks ahead, shedding light on the future of mainframe databases in the context of Big Data and other emerging trends. We tackle the challenges and opportunities of modernizing mainframe databases, offering pragmatic solutions for ensuring their longevity and continued relevance.

In-depth case studies provide real-world context and practical applications of the principles discussed. These examples serve to highlight the diverse sectors where mainframe databases continue to thrive – from banking to healthcare, government institutions, and beyond.

Also by Ricardo Nuqui

Mainframe Knowledge
Mainframe Architecture: An Introduction
Mainframe Computing
Mainframe Cybersecurity: A Comprehensive Guide
Mainframe Networking: An Introduction
Mainframe Operations: An Introduction
Mainframe Systems Programming: An Introduction
Mainframe Storage: An Introduction
Harnessing Mainframe Databases: Strategies for Modern Data
Management
Mainframe Transaction Processing: Principles, Practices, and
Paradigms

Mainframe Use
Mainframes vs Other Platforms: A Pragmatic View

Ingram Content Group UK Ltd.
Milton Keynes UK
UKHW050732220623
423745UK00022B/371

9 789815 164893